What's a Little Wind?

Jon Pirincci

WHAT DOES THIS BOOK HAVE TO DO WITH WIND?

You may be wondering what wind has to do with Inspiration.

It started with an old man in his 80's in an elevator giving advice to a young 32 year old me. Hurricane Andrew was coming, but he was an Auschwitz survivor and this was no comparison to what he went through. In that exact moment I gained instant perspective and how I was inspired.

Millions of people around the world have personal problems and issues to deal with everyday. Some are worse than others, but 95% of them are really not that main of an issue. Think of it like this.

When you are tired of working for your company or boss, you get angry and just hate the world. Think about NOT having a job like millions of others.

You are behind on your rent or mortgage payment and always tight on money. What about the people who are homeless, or staying on a friends couch?

Your stuck in traffic and screaming at the other driver...at least you have a car. Try doing that on a bus.

You have a cold or worse a broken arm or leg...others have a deadly disease and may die sooner than they expected.

You are tired from walking all day for work and other daily activities, then you see a person in a wheelchair.

After you read my book it will help you relate to the daily problems we all have, but you will have support from the top religions, philosophers, and luminaries from around the world.

Each chapter will have phrases to motivate you from the top inspirational-spiritual people along with well know celebrities.

The Bible, Torah, and Quran are also written here on what has been said about the exact situation in each chapter that happened in my life. Most likely, a similar situation in your life also. People have had problems thousands of years ago and similar problems now.

The scriptures here will show proof and validate this.

They also show that all religions convey the same message...love each other and believe in a higher spirit.

Your problems will be like a candle in the wind, flickering but then blown out. It's because of the powers above and the deep wisdom behind it all. If...that is what you want to believe.

It's the way you want to look at your life with out judging others.

When you are in those situations, just relax for a minute and think about this...really...

"What's a little wind?"

I hope you enjoy the book and God Bless.

Jon Pirincci

CONTENTS

ACKNOWLEDGMENTS

I would like to thank all the people who breezed through my life and made this happen with the positive wind behind my back.

First and always first...my family. My dad Alaettin because I was always happy to be known as the doctor's son. He was a well known cardiologist and a religious man. He raised an amazing family with love and support while helping others who were sick but poor and not charge them. He lived an amazing 88 years.

My mother Nebahat who is the angel on earth to me. She also brought me into this world and gave me the wisdom and humor behind life. She is to me an example what all wives and mothers should be.

My brothers Jemal and Deniz... the best brothers a guy can have. You can't go wrong with a doctor who speaks three languages and a real estate investor-business man as your peers and mentors. Oh, they also supported me through hard times, financially and motivating me to be who I am.

Nick Vujicic and his incredible and emotional book "Life with out limits". You will never think life sucks when you read this gem. Thanks Nick.

Joel Bauer, who without him and his motivational seminars there would be no book. Everyone has a book in them, and I have proved it.

I want to also thank speaker and author Annie Armen for her great advice and wisdom that helped me with my book and speaking engagements.

I especially would like to thank Azaan Kamau from Glover Lane Press. She helped spread my positive wind message all over the world on Amazon and Barnes and Noble.

To my great friends and others who I have met in my life and wrote about in my life stories.

All those positive and wonderful writers, philosophers, speakers who have shared their insight to me and millions of others in their quotes.

Tom Shadyac who is the great writer and producer of many top grossing films in Hollywood and the incredible documentary "I AM". My book is inspired by his life and those stories about others.

Oprah Winfrey because of how she struggled through a horrible personal life to creating twenty five years of life changing shows.

Charles Schultz and my favorite "Charlie Brown Christmas". Linus said it all in that speech about what Christmas is all about. 45 years later... still brings tears to my eyes and millions of others also.

PJ McClure with his knowledge and motivation of looking at life in a spiritual way.

Theresa Caputo of "The Medium." Who shows that the ones who passed... are still with us. The stories here also prove that.

I also have to give credit to the wonderful online and book information relating to the individual religious scripture excerpts provided here: The Open Bible, The sayings of Muhammad, Jewish Quotes, UMJC.org, Electic Site.co, Age of the Sage.com, Quod.lib.umich.edu. They provide the insight to the meaning behind the wisdom and beliefs.

And of course....GOD. There is only one...and that's all we need.

1. WHAT'S A LITTLE WIND?

The date of August 24th, 1992 was a very life changing date for me, and millions of others. I don't just mean that in a materialistic way of billions of dollars in destruction from 150 mile an hour winds. It does not mean that this hurricane changed the way the US reacted to future tropical storms and the way FEMA budgeted their system in helping others in a life crisis like this. No… this has more of a personal story to this. A personal story between me and a man from a different generation. A true witness to how some people respond to certain situations compared to others reacting to the same one.

A few days before Hurricane Andrew hit Homestead Florida I was thinking of what I should do to escape these colossal winds. Do I go back to Orlando and get away even though I just moved from there a week before? Maybe the weather man was wrong and it won't be as bad as everyone said it will be. I have heard this many times, just did not know what to do. I never went through a Hurricane before. The worst thing that had ever happened to me was having hail fall on my car and sometimes on my head, and that hurt.

So I decided to stay and wait it out. Then something happened that put all this and other things in my life in perspective. Something that stayed with me 22 years later.

I decided to stay and see what the world had in store for me. I was living at my parent's condo in North Miami Beach Florida right on the ocean. They had bought it back in the 1970's and I went there every year for vacation and family time.

Their condo was on the 9th floor and of course you took a nice elevator to get there. I waited for that elevator to arrive thinking it would be empty because maybe the whole building would be almost empty. A hurricane was coming! Well I was wrong... and I'm glad I was.

There was a man who must have been in his 80's going to his floor also. Being the friendly neighbor I am, I was just wondering what this man thought of this huge hurricane coming to pummel us with 150 mile an hour winds. He asked me in his very heavy accented Polish voice what floor I was going to. I said ninth floor please. We were on our way until I just had to ask him what he thought about the hurricane coming. Yes... I can be persistent at times, especially under stress. He just looked at me and smiled... said nothing. Then I asked again if he was scared that something might happen to his family or condo. Maybe the furniture on the balcony would fall in the water. The windows would break... so many things went through my mind. Then this man said something funny, well... so I thought. I asked him again what he was going to do. He said "Well... hurricane shmuricane". I said to myself, what?. Did he just say that? Obviously this did not make him worry or get upset. I asked him why? After a small pause of him staring at me and thinking why I was asking such personal questions to a man I never met before he said "Do you know what I went though many, many years ago"? I was thinking he went through another major storm like this one. So I asked him...what? With a gleam in his eye and an assertiveness I don't ever see in too many older men his age I impatiently waited for the answer. He finally said... Auschwitz!

Obviously knowing the tragic history about one of the worst events of mankind, it made me stunned and wondered about what he just said. I looked at him intently and just said... "Oh". Then my mind was thinking what are the chances of all the people I would talk to on this particular day, time and place to hear this. As he looked at me knowing what I was thinking he rolled up his sleeve and showed me his numbers tattooed on his lower right arm above the wrist. While I looked at this in shock he said something to me that stayed in my mind for the past 22 years referring to the hurricane, "WHATS A LITTLE WIND?"

I thought about what he just said and it all made sense in a matter of seconds. He is right, he was a survivor of some event that most people did not survive. Depending on your past life experiences, that is how we should all look at life. "WHATS A LITTLE WIND?"

The older and very wise man then went out the elevator to his floor, winked and said… have great life son.

So now I am thinking how wise he was for saying that? When we all have bad days we must stay happy. Things in life can always be worse… always!

The moral of this chapter and the book is life's main vision.

Whenever anything bothers you, and it's just one of those days, just think about those four little words that will change your outlook on that day and hopefully… the rest of your life.

* * *

"What's a little future with no worries? That means that we all should live everyday with gratitude and not worry about the future.

"I do not want to foresee the future. I am concerned with taking care f the present. God has given me no control over the moment following". -Mahatma Gandhi

"The main goal of the future is to stop violence. The world is addicted to it." -Bill Cosby

"You cant connect the dots looking forward;,you can only connect them looking backwards. So you have to trust that the dots will somehow connect in your future. You have to trust in something-your gut,destiny,life,karma,whatever. This approach has never let me down,and it ha made all the difference in my life." - Steve Jobs

"Stop acting as if life is a rehearsal. Live this day as if it were your last. The past is over and gone. The future is not guaranteed." -Dr Wayne Dyer

"Be careful what you water your dreams with. Water them with worry and fear you will produce weeds that choke the life from your dream. Water them with optimism and solutions and you will cultivate success" - Lao Tzu

2. THE CURRENT OF LIFE

My whole life I wanted to go to different tropical places like Tahiti, Bahamas and Maui. All my friends that went there would brag to me about how they had so much fun in the sand and ocean.

The temperature would be perfect in the air and water. There is nothing better than swimming in an ocean when you don't get cold. Florida is like that. I know because I lived in Miami for six years. The ocean in Hawaii and other areas are even warmer. Nothing better than snorkeling and diving down there.

So one day in 1986 I had a chance to go to Honolulu, Hawaii with my friends. I worked for a great home remodeling company called Master Home Remodeling in Rochester, NY. It's a great name and has a strong meaning which I will explain later. We sold siding, windows, roofing and other products for the home. I was on a team of canvassers that walked for hours trying to set up appointments for the sales people to sell the owners. We would walk in the middle of the snow, rain then blazing heat. We would do this all throughout the year. Our company was one of the top producers in selling these products to our wholesalers that provide it to us. When you sell a certain amount of volume, the company sends you on certain trips around the USA for FREE. That's right… plane, hotel and most of your travel expenses for a certain amount of people in the office. In my case… I went with two other friends. We won a trip to Honolulu.

Now we were in our 20's so all we cared about was partying and chasing girls, which we did. We stayed at a great hotel in the center of the city, the Hilton. The best part of the vacation was renting mopeds and driving around the city. Me and the guys also rented a nice truck to drive around from beach to beach. After we found the beaches, we asked the locals about swimming there. Not the places where the usual tourists from Cleveland go. These were the dangerous beaches that you only go to if you know about them and if you are an excellent swimmer. They even had signs saying to "not to swim and be careful because of the strong tides!

Well you know how people think when on vacation. They think nothing will happen to them. I have been swimming my whole life starting at five years old. I have swam in the beaches of the Bahamas, Puerto Rico, Ft. Lauderdale and many more. What was I going to be scared about here? Just before that we also went snorkeling and swimming near dolphins and other areas around the south side of the island.

So here I am. With my best friends Pete and John all ready to dive in and enjoy the ocean where others have gone. Only if you were a local and great swimmer should you be here. It was about 2 pm, 80 degrees, and the waves were pretty large and wide. I started swimming farther and farther away from the beach. My good friend John was just a few yards away from me doing the same thing. Pete was on the beach watching us look like kids in a damn pool. We were there not knowing what is going to happen next. What I am about to write here made absolutely no sense to me or my friends, but it did happen!.

While I am about fifty feet from the shore I realize that I am getting tired. I'm swimming straight to the beach as strong and as fast as I can. That way I can stand on the beach and relax. My friend John oddly enough was thinking the same exact thing. He was also getting tired and he was about two hundred twenty pounds to my one hundred and fifty.

While I was trying to get back I noticed that I was not moving one foot closer to the beach from five minutes earlier. I just could not figure it out. No reason at all. Not only was I getting tired trying to get back the waves, they were getting larger and stronger hitting me on the head and shoulders. Inside the waves were also parts of sand and coral scraping my body. I looked again to my friend John and he was yelling at me "Jon… I can't get back!" I replied "I know… neither can I!" We screamed at Pete and he was smiling thinking nothing was happening to us. He did not see the worry and sheer terror we were going through. So I tried to not panic and just kept swimming and swimming until I could not anymore. It was about 15 minutes, maybe twenty, I was getting exhausted and was swallowing the ocean water preventing me to breath. I was so tired and disorientated… I just really did not know what to do.

I was now thinking… I was going to die! I thought about my mom and dad and two brothers. That I would hear from them the way I died was senseless. Drowning? How could that be? I'm in good shape, I have swam for twenty years before and was even on the high school swimming team like my brother Deniz. "Please God… don't let this happen!" So that is exactly what I did. I prayed to the Lord to help me. To just guide me back to the beach. Show me what to do. "Please God help!"

Now here is the amazing part of how I was saved. The second that I prayed and said that, I somehow decided to swim to the right, parallel to the shore. Why? I have no idea. I just thought maybe that I was in a current that was stopping me from going to the beach. Maybe, maybe not.

So I swam to the right a few yards and then straight. Right again and straight. As I was doing that while trying to not swallow the water and still getting hit on the head by the force of the waves, something happened. I was getting closer to the shore. Then the waves stopped slamming into me as much as it was before. I was getting free. I was catching my breath and saw the shore just a few yards away from me! Not fifty feet, not thirty, not even twenty… but right next to where Pete was enjoying himself getting a darn tan! I also looked over to my left and wondered about my friend John. Where was he? Did he drown? Did he follow what I did? Where was John?? I looked over and saw his head bob from under the water. Then his shoulders, then his whole body. He made it! He was right next to me.

John also had an amazing story. When he was almost drowning like I was, he also prayed to be saved. I thought he swam to the right side like I did and the currents stopped. That's not what happened. Something even more amazing did. Within seconds of his prayer he felt sand underneath his feet.

He thought it was just the current mixing up the sand. No… the shore came up under his feet without being closer the shore! It must have been a sand hill that just happened to be there from the currents when John needed it. Amazing huh?

We both came to the shore absolutely one hundred percent totally exhausted and at exactly the same time. I have never been so tired in my life and thought I was going to have a heart attack, but I was alive! I made it. John made it! Life is good again!

We then explained the story to our good friend Pete and he just did not believe it. He knew we were trying to get back to the shore, but did not know how bad the situation was. We spent a few more days there and headed back to cold miserable Rochester, NY in the dead of winter.

While watching TV one night I saw a program about safety. Different situations in emergencies. How to survive in fires, hurricanes, car crashes and... preventing drowning! As I watched in suspense about what they were going to say about preventing a drowning, I was shocked at what they said, especially in an ocean! They showed that if you were caught in waves and tides like I was. I was to "swim to the side". Yes that's right, "swim to a side, left or right".

The reason is that the ocean has tides and eddies that are created from the ocean floor to the water above. When you swim to an angle or the sides, you will catch certain flows of water that have "No tides or eddies". That's what happened to John and I!

The exact and specific time I prayed to God to help me, he did. It's as if he took my body and lifted it to the perfect part of the ocean where there were absolutely no tides and the waves there would push me towards the beach. What are the chances of that? Okay... maybe I got lucky, but when one prays, the luckier they get! Then I found out that John my friend did the exact same thing. He prayed for help and got it.

Oh...I also told what happened to other people that I worked at Master Home Remodeling. Especially the owner Dave who happened to be a strict and devout Christian.

When I mentioned this to him he just looked at me with a slight smile and gleam in his eye. He mentioned something to me I never knew until my almost drowning incident happened. The way Dave came up with the name MASTER home remodeling was this. Not to be a MASTER home remodeler... NO! Not the MASTER in business. No!... his Master meant... GOD.

When I shared this story with others, they thought the same thing. It was not my time to go and I had a reason to live! I was born to be a comedian-actor and speaker. That's why I am still here twenty eight years later still pursuing my dream and trying to help others.

I also found out recently that the famous Grammy Award winning singer Cat Stevens (Yusef Islam) had the exact life changing situation off the coast of Malibu in 1976. He was drowning and said if God helped him survive, he would spread the word of Islam. A wave came a few seconds after and pushed him ashore. Amazing... right?

Which is why I am sharing this story with you!

* * *

What's a little guidance? A lot in many ways when it comes from Heaven above!

"Accept the things to which fate binds you, and love the people with whom fate brings you together, but do so with all your heart." -Marcus Aurelius

"One life is all we have and we live it as we believe in living it. But to sacrifice what you are and to live without belief, that is a fate more terrible than dying." -Joan of Arc

"Norman Day, let me be aware of the treasure you are. Let me learn from you, love you, bless you before you depart. Let me not pass you by in the quest of some perfect tomorrow". -Mary Jean Irion

3. UNCLE SAM

Uncle Sam means so much to so many people in different ways. To some its an uncle in your family. To others it is a metaphor for our great country, the good ole USA.

You know some of the quotes you have heard the past many years. "Sorry about the sales tax Mr. Jones, we all got to pay Uncle Sam." Or… "Those boys going to war for Uncle Sam, God Bless them!"

Well to me, it meant that and more. There was a living breathing symbol of what America was and some parts, still is. His name was Sam Manuse.

When I was ten years old living in Rochester, NY back in the 1970's, Sam was my neighbor across the street. A man with a dynamic personality, humor and genuine concern for people. The kind of neighbor everyone wants and actually needs these days. You see, Sam was a war hero, from the Big One, WWII as he said in his loud rotund voice that you can hear from across the street and a block way.

He was a true Italian, his parents were from Sicily. He had a nice family, a wife and two lovely daughters Patricia and Phyllis. He had no boys, and knowing that I felt like I was his surrogate son. You know, the son he never had but always wanted. That's how I got to know him so well.

You see Sam and his family would invite me, my parents, and two older brothers the first Sunday of the month, every month for an old fashioned home cooked Italian lunch. This went on for years. We would have the best lasagna and meatballs dinner you could ever have, even to this day. This traditional, old school Italian would scream at the top of his lungs, "Eat Jonny, eat! It will put hair on your chest!" as he cackled out loud with a laugh. Now that statement he made really scared me, remember I was just 10 years old. I didn't want hair on my chest as a preteen ten year old, that was weird! I could see if I was maybe fifteen or sixteen and started dating, but not at ten. Everyone also had two to three helpings and had that stuffed feeling where you could barely walk.

Then after we had the traditional pasta, we were just about to have our favorite desert from Mrs. Manuse. Sam would start telling us about his combat days in WWII. The one that I remembered the best was when he spent time in Italy. He and his "Boys" as he affectionately called them, were surrounded by Germans. They did not have anywhere to go until he looked down the mountain and noticed a small abandoned farm house. They ran and hid there not moving an inch because the enemy Germans were just a few feet away. They were also hungry and hadn't eaten for days until Sam noticed something in another house 20 yards away. It was a few cans of beans. As I ate my desert of chocolate cake and apple pie, I listened intently to every single word. Uncle Sam would explain to his small Sunday audience and then he would scream to me "Jonny," not Jon, and after a few glasses of beer "Giovanni". Before he began I knew I was in for a colorful treatment of sound effects and emotion. With my Uncle Sam, you did not just listen to a story, you lived it!

"You see Jonny, here I was on top of this mountain hiding behind this little old house. The war was in full force and me and the boys haven't eaten in a few days, we were tired and weak and starvin'. "Bombs and missiles flying over our heads boom, Ba Boom, missing us by inches." I was thinking it seemed like the 4th of July at a dining room table.

Then once in a while not to scare this ten year old boy, he would cackle that infectious laugh while still explaining how the war sounded. "The machine guns were going Rata tat tat… and bombs BOOM!!.

"I did not care and ran to get those beans. It was either die of hunger, get shot, or try to eat". So I said, "then what happened Uncle Sam, then what?" In my little voice you have before you hit puberty.

"I made it to the cans after the shooting went silent and we got lucky to have one of the best meals in our lives. I shared it with the boys and they never forgot it. Not only that, by the grace from the man upstairs we got taken in by an Italian woman that saw us and even gave us more food".

"Is that how it really happened Sam? Really"? "That's the way it was in the big one... WWII!" as I saw the expression in his eyes like he was reliving those awful painful days.

After our lunch he went upstairs to show us his medal of honor he got from the general. He was not showing off, but more of a sense of pride. Sam even showed the bullet scars he had from the mountain story. It was in his back left leg. Years later I understood why he could not walk well when it was cold or rainy. In Rochester, it's like that very often.

As I remembered those times at my home across the street from Sam, I realized just how important and significant to have a real Uncle Sam. Especially these days.

As the years went by I would help Sam. Like the time I was cutting his yard with my parents riding mower. He would slip me a five dollar bill in my little hand, almost like he was embarrassed to show his kindness. I tried to refuse but he just crunched it in my hand and walked away with a smile.

Sam always returned the favor though. It would snow many feet every winter and my whole family would be snowed in. Sometimes it would take days for the local driveway service to come and clear us out so my dad could go to work. Dad was a cardiologist and was very well respected in the community. The Uncle would be there at eight am on a Sunday to make sure we could get out.

Sunday at eight a.m.! Other times he would take us to the airport when we went on vacation. I mean, who does that anymore?

One of my best memories growing up is when I asked my parents if they could let me see Santa Claus. It was Christmas and I wanted my new Rockem Sockem Robots, remember them? So one night a few days before Christmas I actually did see Santa. He came over to my house and put me on his knee yelling HO HO HO. I looked up at Santa and told him all the things I wanted but noticed one thing. Santa's glasses and voice sounded just like... Sam. Mom and Dad never told me it was, so I just kept believing like all children do. At ten years old, who does not want to believe in Santa?

Well Uncle Sam is gone now, more than thirty years. At his funeral he had his many friends from the Veteran of Foreign Wars there to pay their respects. I was there too with my mom, dad and two brothers. I was older then, about 23 when he passed away from health issues.

I remember that I could not help asking one of his good Veteran Friends if he served with Sam. With tears in his eyes, raising his head and looking up." Yes… he was one of the good ones". I also got teary eyed.

Now as I go and visit my childhood home every Thanksgiving, I cannot forget the great memories as I glaze across the street. It was about a man called Sam. My Uncle Sam.

In all fairness, he was not my real uncle. Not in a way that reflects family heritage and relatives. He was just synonymous with Courage, Friendship, Decency, Old Fashioned Values and above all… respect. The things that make living in America Great.

The Uncle I never really had, but the one we all want and need… an Uncle Sam.

* * *

So…*What's a little Patriotism?* It's everything we live for. God Bless America.

"These fallen heroes represent the character of a nation who has a long history of patriotism and honor-and a nation who has fought many battles to keep our country free from threats of terror" -Michael N Castle

"Patriotism is easy to understand in America. It means looking out for yourself by looking out for your country" -Calvin Coolidge

"We the people recognize that we have responsibilities as well as rights, that our destinies are bound together, that a freedom which only asks what's in it for me, a freedom with out a commitment to others, a freedom without love or charity or duty or patriotism, is unworthy of our founding ideals and those who died in their defense." -Barack Obama

"137 years later, Memorial Day remains one of Americas most cherished patriotic observances. The spirit of this day has not changed-it remains a day to honor those who died defending our freedom and democracy." -Doc Hastings

4. THE NUMBERS THAT CHANGED LIVES

Over the past 25 years I have talked to many people who have traveled around the world. They have gone to Paris, Hong Kong, Hawaii, Italy, the very top tourist destinations. On top of this list is also Istanbul, Turkey. Oprah did a special a few years ago on travel, and said that also. I have had a chance to travel there many times over the years and always loved it. I also have relatives there so that always helps and cuts down on expenses like hotels and restaurants. You see it's an insult if you travel there and NOT stay with your extended Turkish family. That's why I went to visit Istanbul back in August/September of 2001.

It all started when my favorite cousin Ella announced she was getting married to her long time boyfriend Murat. This was exciting news to all of us, especially my mom and dad. So we all decided to make this a family event and travel to Istanbul to celebrate her wedding.

I was in Los Angeles so I wanted to go to NYC and see my brother Jemal to travel together on the same flight. When I got there, I forgot just how beautiful Manhattan was with Times Square, Central Park and of course the Twin Towers. I haven't been to New York for many years before that, and could not wait to sight see a little. So we did many things there before we went to Turkey. The one spot I wanted to go to really bad was the Twin Towers. It was back in the 1980's the last time I went and just loved the view up there. So I told my brother that we should go there and have fun. He said in his cocky attitude, that he went there many times and "it's not going anywhere Jon, we can go some other time". Man was he wrong!

So we took off to Turkey, but had to do an 11 hour layover in Amsterdam. That was okay because we did the boat tours on the canals, had great food and of course the famous Red Light district. After the sights there, we were ready to catch our night flight to beautiful Istanbul. This is the only country that is on the European AND Asian continents. I could not wait!

So we enter Turkey late at night and take a taxi to our aunt's apartment that is very nice and overlooks the Bosphorous. You see ships from Russia, Poland, even China taking cargo and also tourists.

Over the next few days we had fun with my whole family including my other brother Deniz and his wife and two kids. We ate at amazing restaurants on the Black Sea, took boat tours, went to the Grand Bazzar, and of course the absolutely incredible Blue Mosque. The Turkish people are always very nice to any tourists from every country. They don't care about other people's religions or beliefs because that is just not the way people are there. They will treat you with respect no matter what you do or who you are. I really found this out a few days later.

After enjoying ourselves the past few days and of course the amazing wedding for Ella and all our relatives, we needed a few home cooked meals. About 5:30 pm on a nice September night we were eating a delicious home cooked meal consisting of Borek, Rice with Yogurt and of course Kofte with onions and parsley. Kofte is ground hamburger. We were all laughing and talking about the great times we were having there. Then we get a phone call from my brother's friend. Jemal almost did not take the call because it's rude when you're eating dinner, but this was different. His friend said we need to turn on CNN and watch what's happening in NYC. My brother said NYC? It's 9 a.m. there, what could be going on? We turn on the TV and see a plane hitting some building. Then we see it's not just any building, it's the Twin Towers.

At first we thought it was movie or some kind of documentary, but no it was 9-11!

Like millions of others in the US and Turkey, we were just shocked and did not know what was happening there. Was it an accident? Terrorists? Just did not know until later in the news cast.

As I found out about this attack and then finding out another tower was going down, I almost fainted with sadness and disbelief. I cried in the bathroom looking at the mirror thinking how could this happen? Why did God let this happen? I needed answers. I then went back to the table and looked at my parents. My dad said he thought he would not ever see anything like this in his lifetime. My mom said the same thing. Both are very religious and strict Muslims also. We were all just there not knowing what to think.

The next day we tried to carry on as normal as possible, even though we knew we could not. My brother Deniz and his family actually went back just two days before 9-11 took place. I was there with my brother most of the time while my mom and dad were ready to go back to Rochester, NY. We all had different plans and flights. While we were there we were talking to the other local Turks about how they felt on what was happening in America. We were a little nervous because we did not know what most of the people were thinking. Even though earlier in the vacation there were no issues among the US and Middle East countries like Turkey. You see, 90% of Turkey are Muslim. Americans are mostly Christian, Catholic and other religions. The terrorists that hit the Towers were of course Muslims that were dedicated to Islam. When we talked about this to the taxi drivers, the guy who runs the photo shop, waiters in the restaurants, we thought that they would say since we were Americans that were not Muslim we deserved it. My brother and I did not say we were Muslims, but just Americans that knew Turkish. A few days more we were ready to go back to the US… so we thought. That's right, the US stopped the flights and all airlines were grounded. We were really nervous now… when are we getting back? Then of course I got lucky and the date I was supposed to fly back was when America decided to let planes fly again. I was also flying back to JFK airport in New York City!

I got on the flight thinking everyone will be talking about 9-11 and how terrible the Muslim faith is. How Islam was a horrible religion and no one should be involved in that… ever. I kept quiet and got to JFK. I had breakfast in the hotel they placed me in so I can leave the next morning. I overheard the conversations. I heard what the armed guards were saying. The hotel staff. My waiter, hostess. Everyone was talking about the religions and why this happened. I found out after listening, and of course the news that it's NOT the Muslim religion.

It's the individual people involved. It's like that in every situation when it involves religious activities! I knew one of the first verses the Quran says is "never harm anyone at any time... EVER." Killing is one of the worst sins you can do. I also knew that the Bible and Torah said the same thing. How do people be so hurtful on religions when bad things happen?

So now its thirteen years later and we are still having issues with this topic. Religions, what's the best? What's the worst? Should I convert to another? Okay maybe you will just not believe in any God or spiritual existence. Well here is the answer. All religions are good... all are great... all send the same message. Be a good person, believe in a higher being and help and love each other with no previous judgments... ever! It's actually a very simple concept isn't it? Well it can be, if you let it.

* * *

What's a little Prejudice? It's something that should not exist in our lives... ever!

"Rivers, ponds, lakes and streams-they all have different names, but they all contain water. Just as religions do.-they all contain truths". -Muhammad Ali

"This is my simple religion. There is no need for temples; no need for complicated philosophy. Our own brain, our own heart is our temple; the philosophy is kindness". -Dalai Lama

"I love you when you bow in your mosque, kneel in your temple, pray in your church. For you and I are sons of one religion, and it is the spirit." -Khalil Gibran

"A just laicism allows religious freedom. The state does not impose religion but rather gives space to religions with a responsibility toward civil society, and therefore it allows these religions to be factors in building up society." -Pope Benedict XVI

5. THE BIRD AND THE CHAIR

Ever hear about how spirits of the deceased come back to show they are still alive? Theresa Caputo of "The Medium" show proves this every week.

This is one amazing true story of the close relationship between a mother, her daughter and what doctors thought would never happen.

One of the closest friends I have is a great person name Pete Harper. I have known him since the old days when friendships actually meant something. I am talking over thirty years ago from Rochester, NY. He moved to San Diego to pursue other ambitions he had in business, and of course the beautiful weather. He and I have always liked dating women, but deep down inside we both wanted to get married and have kids. I am still waiting for this, but Pete found his soul mate back in the early 90's. He met her in a nightclub of all places. Her name is Sandra and she is from an old fashioned Mexican family from Tijuana. What I mean by Old Fashioned, is the nice family she was brought up with. Like when going on the first few dates with Peter, they actually had a chaperone who was a relative come with her. A chaperone, no one does that anymore! The two eventually fell in love and married a few years later. I was at the wedding and had a chance to meet Sandra's mom and dad and the rest of her siblings. Many years before, I knew Peter's family back in New York.

I loved her parents because they reminded me of mine. Especially her mom. You know, sweet and nice and always protective of her children and others also. They actually lived with her for a few years as they were getting on in age. Her dad was hard working in different jobs while her mom had the toughest job one can have... being a Mexican mother!

As the years went by, her parents got older and sick with diseases. Dad passed away and just a few years later, her mom did too, the year was 1998. She unfortunately had a heart attack from some health issues, and after trying to save her from placing tubes and other medicine, it just did not work. While she was in the hospital, many of her family came to see her to pay respects and pray. Pete was there, friends and many others that even came from Tijuana and other cities many hours away. Sandra was there every night. I did not know this was happening or I would have come also.

While Sandra was there, she would talk to her mother and not just pray for her, but to ask her to never let her down by not keeping in touch with her. The doctors were there also and did not want to get Sandra more upset and depressed, but wanted to mention something to her. In many cases when you talk to someone in a bad condition like Sandra's mom, usually that person cannot hear or understand what you are saying. There have been many documents and instances that show proof of this, but not this time. Usually is the key word here. Sandra did not listen to the doctors. She did not care about the many other times that patients could not hear a family member talk. She talked every day believing in all her heart that her beloved mother would respond to her wonderful and spiritual daughter's request. The story now becomes amazing.

Two days after her mom passed away Sandra was at home working on her real estate investing company with her husband Peter. It was a normal day working upstairs in the office sitting in her large heavy black chair at the computer. She would also go downstairs to take care of her children and other household needs and then continue to work in the office again. While sitting there at the computer typing away she noticed something extremely strange in the office. She did not know what was about to happen, because it was just so fast. A bird with very bright blue feathers flew into the room and circled around Sandra's neck brushing its feathers on her. It swooped slowly, but with purpose around her neck twice and then stopped. As she watched in shock and amazement, she wanted to help the bird fly outside, but could not. The bird was not there anymore. Gone!

So she thought that it must have gone through the window, but the window was closed. It was winter outside and she never opened the window when it was cloudy and cold like that. How did this happen and why? Was the bird lost and maybe, just maybe, it was in the office before Sandra started working? No one knows, so the day went on as usual.

The second day was normal as usual. Some of the workers came in to get paperwork from Sandra and Peter to go to the job sites that needed work. Pete was there for a few minutes but left with the other workers. While Sandra was going upstairs to work, she noticed something very strange. She could not enter the office because her large and heavy black office chair was under the entrance to the doorway. She did not put the chair there, who did? No one else was in the upstairs office. The chair was also moved from way across the office, about 15 feet, on its own and landed right where you entered the upstairs and door entrance. She is thinking again, what is happening? Now she is very confused and was going to tell her husband and others that the house may be haunted, or with a strange feeling around it. Instead, Sandra was thinking, could it be her mom doing this? Is it true? She just moved on and wanted to see if it really was. Then it happened again… the very next day!

The fourth day was again something that many people who don't believe in "the other side" could comprehend. It was payday at the Harper house and checks had to be written for that week's work. As the computer was being turned on and the specific accounting software getting ready to be used, another strange incident happened. This was one that just makes no logical sense at all. As this woman from an old fashioned Mexican family was ready to type in the names and amount owed to some of the workers, she noticed certain letters put together. Letters that Sandra has seen many times over the years from her family, especially her sweet mother. While looking at one of the checks she saw this… xxxooo. Translation, hugs and kisses.

We all have seen this before from friends and family and of course when you're in love with someone. But someone who passed away and it was never supposed to happen?

So Sandra immediately wanted to see if this was somehow a technical computer mistake. She tried to type in the xxoo by herself a few times… and she couldn't! She then showed her husband and few others… nothing. They could not do it either. Everyone just could not understand what was going on except of course, Sandra. You see, she started to remember what was said to her mother just a few short days ago. The conversation that was never supposed to happen. The one that doctors said was a waste of time. This whole time it was the loving old fashioned mother of six that could not leave her daughter alone. The one that was always there for her family and friends. She heard everything that Sandra said and wanted to make sure she would always be there for her… always.

So to this day, my wonderful dear wife of my great friend Peter is never worried about what her parents are doing, and if they exist on the other side of heaven. They do! They always have, and will be there for her. So no one should ever worry either when a loved one passes. Never. They exist and are there for you. Always!

* * *

What's a little Spirit? It belongs in all of us…now and when we are gone.

Men fear death as children fear to go into the dark: and as that natural fear in children is increased by tales, so is the other. -Francis Bacon

"No one wants to die. Even people who want to go heaven don't want to die to get there. And yet death is the destination we all share. No one has ever escaped it. And that is as it should be, because death is very likely the single best invention of life. It is life's change agent. It clears out the old to make way for the new" -Steve Jobs

"What we have done for ourselves alone dies with us: what we have done for others and the world remains and is immoral." -Albert Pike

"When I was a child I thought I saw an angel. It had wings and kinda looked like my sister. I opened the door so light could come in the room, and it sort of faded away. My mother said it was probably my Guardian Angel." -Denzel Washington

6. TRUE LOVE… KISMET

Over the years I would ask my parents how they met each other and stay married for almost 65 years. I mean these days with the divorce rate at 50% or more, most don't last 65 DAYS. I was fascinated and impressed when I heard their story. When you read this chapter, I hope you will understand also.

You see my parents met back in the early 1940's in Istanbul, Turkey. Yes, I'm 100% Turkish but somehow along the way ended with an Italian sounding name and physical looks of a made "wise guy". Many times people would come up to me and say "How you doin'?" "Did I see you on the freakin' Sopranos?" Then I would look at them and talk like Joe Pesci "What's a matter with you… huh?"

My father Alaettin came from a very poor family in Izmir, Turkey. His father worked for the government as a civil servant. Dad's mother was a house wife (women did not work back then, especially in Turkey). He had older and younger brothers and sisters who went their own way in life, but dad wanted to be a doctor. So just being from a very poor family and having the motivation to study medicine is amazing, even now in 2014 it's damn hard.

So he made his way to college and medical school in Istanbul. He learned French and English along the way also. So as he got older and was studying hard to be a success in life, he also wanted to get married and have a family.

One day he was walking with some friends and heard one of them talk about a pretty brown haired girl called Nebahat. Some of his friends knew her and her sister also.

They were at a park walking and drinking coffee while the future doctor made his way to talk with her. My mom was nice and talked, but not that interested at the time. Now just to let you know, women did not date many guys at the time, if any. It was just not the way back then... Even in the US it was not like it is now. Remember the show Happy Days?

My gosh... after the third date these days men and women would, well you know.

So as time went by week after week month after month, the relationship between them got stronger. The funny thing my mother would tell me is that she was not sure she wanted to be married to a man who was very poor. She was raised in an upper middle class family. Her dad was a captain of the ships that sailed on the Black Sea and Bosphorous. Her brothers were lawyers and very successful. What is she going to do with this short green eyed man who wants to possibly be a doctor? I later found out that it was not about the money... it was if he was a good man. Mom actually would pay dad $100 a month when she had to help him with bills, rent and succeed in his dreams of being a fine doctor. One hundred dollars in 1946! That was a lot of money back then, it even is now to most people. All my mother wanted was someone who would be a good husband and father someday, that's it. Women actually thought like that back then. Really? Yes!

As the years went by, my father would not see her that often because he was in school studying and she was a teacher in a different city. She ended up being in a city up north near Russia. Dad was not sure how to get a hold of her, but did get an address from her father to send letters and love notes. Yes... you heard right, love notes and poems. It really existed back then. Mom would get these every few weeks and love them so much she could not wait to see him again. He finally went to the school where she was teaching and asked her to go for a walk while the other students were on recess. They wanted privacy, so as they walked away from the school they were talking and possibly planning out their life. Oh... now most people think there was a lot of holding hands and heavy kissing. NO there wasn't. Again, that's not the way it was back then. So when they were walking they did not suspect some of the students were following them and spying to see what would happen. They were. But my parents did nothing but talk.

Finally they decided to set a date to get married. But it was not that easy. You had to get permission from both parents. As the story went on (depending on who I heard it from, Mom or Dad) it took a lot of convincing from Dad and his parents. Where will they marry? When? Who will pay? Okay... Mom's rich father paid. So it all happened in Istanbul Turkey August 12th, 1948.

Later on my two brothers were born. Jemal in Istanbul 1949 and Deniz in 1956. Though there was a separation between them because my dad got a letter saying they needed doctors in the United States. So he left my mother there with my brother as dad pursued his dream of being a great doctor of cardiology. Well they ended up being in Colorado where Deniz was born, then Seattle, Washington where I was born in 1960. The best part of the story is this. After dad got to America, his luck got better and better. His pay got more and more. The lives he provided for his wife and kids were nothing my mom imagined when she met that short green eyed poor man many years before. It all happened after I was born dad told me. Oh... shucks!

By the 1970's in Rochester NY, my proud father who just wanted to follow his dream and be a doctor got married to his true love and had three smart healthy kids. He also became a certified cardiologist. He helped many of the people that could not sometimes afford to go to a doctor, and went to him for free. My brother Deniz took over his practice to keep the family legacy going when he retired in 1992. It's been over twenty years now.

We went on vacations to Puerto Rico, Bahamas, Germany, and got a beautiful condo in North Miami Beach, Florida right on the ocean and waterways. Mom had all the things she never thought she would have being this little school girl from Turkey. My parents were the best. Unfortunately Dad passed away in 2007, but mom is still here healthy and happy as can be. I call her my Angel on Earth!

So when you really think about why people get married and how, it's the things that think matter, but do not. It's not about money. Yes it helps, but it's not what keeps people together. It's not totally about looks either. You now see these tall guys with their six pack abs and driving their BMWs. That is again NOT what keeps women happy and married for 65 years.

It's about the person inside. Inside! The heart, the soul, personality, manners, judgment, honesty, and sheer determination to love just that one person. Only that ONE person… forever. That is what true love is.

* * *

What's a little love? By reading this chapter I hope you think… everything you make it to be and more.

"Sometimes the heart sees what is invisible to the eye" -H. Jackson Brown Jr.

"Where there is love there is life" -Mahatma Gandhi

"If you live to be a hundred, I want to live to be a hundred minus one day so I never have to live without you" -A.A. Milne

"Love begins at home, and its how much we do…but how much love we put in action" -Mother Teresa

7. A SURVIVOR OF FAITH

A Personal Story by Olivia Masui

Hello, my name is Olivia Masui and I am 30 years old. I live in Orange County, CA with my husband, Kevin. I teach English to Korean people and Kevin works in the IT field.

From birth, I have always been raised in a strong Christian household. My parents brought me and my brother to church regularly and raised us with good values. We have always known that God loves us. As my teenage years approached, I began to associate with "the wrong crowd" and my relationship with God was dwindling. When I was about 15 or 16, I said a doubtful prayer. It went something like this: "God, if you're listening to me and if I'm not talking to myself, please reveal yourself to me. I can't afford to screw up my one chance at salvation."

As a teenager, my name was Olivia Van Leuven. On January 1st, 2000, I was driving to my boyfriend's house and I lost control of my vehicle. I was 16 at that time. Bystanders later told my parents that my car just drifted across the center divider into oncoming traffic. Some suggested that my brakes stopped working. Another theory proposed to my parents was that my huge 1985 Chevy Blazer hit black ice, because it had just rained. I wasn't intoxicated and I didn't fall asleep so, to this day, we don't know what happened. People also told my parents that they had seen another person in the car with me. I believe this was my guardian angel.

I had suffered a severe Traumatic Brain Injury, or TBI. The

Glasgow Coma Scale is rated from a 3 to a 15, with a 15 being completely normal, healthy, and awake, and a 3 being completely brain dead. I was rated as a 4.

As I lay in the hospital bed with every bone broken, my dad's friend said to him "She will graduate from high school."

After one month at Enloe hospital in a coma, I was transported to Kentfield Rehabilitation hospital in Central CA. When I awoke, I couldn't see, talk, move, and part of my head was shaved. My right side was contracted and atrophied. Because I had no recollection of anything at all, because there was a covering around my bed (resembling a cage to prevent me from falling out), and because my vision was extremely blurry, I assumed that I must be dreaming. Utterly terrified, I turned to God, begging him to wake me up. On top of that, I wore a huge neck brace that prevented me from moving my head. This "dream" lasted for about two weeks (because I had no concept of time) and I thought that if the neck brace came off, I would come out of the dream. I tore it off several times, but I didn't wake up. One of my first true memories is seeing a calendar on the wall in my room – it said March 2nd. It's my birthday soon, I thought. My birthday is on March 11th.

I came home on May 3rd. I returned to high school and graduated on time with my class. I went on to attend California State University, Chico and graduated with a Bachelor of Arts degree in Linguistics.

It took me six years to earn my Bachelor's degree (if only I had known that Linguistics is one of the most difficult majors offered by the university). I chose the Linguistics major because I was trying to avoid any major that would involve any sort of math. Because the left frontal lobe of my brain had been damaged, and because math/analytical processes are mainly conducted in the left hemisphere, my math/analytical skills were nearly gone.

I would have to say that the most difficult part of this whole experience has been the social aspect. The boyfriend whose house I was driving to the evening of the accident left, as did nearly everyone else. For a 16-year-old girl, friends and acceptance is highly important. All throughout college and my remaining time in high school, I was VERY odd. Everyone avoided me and walked away when they saw me. I would have done *anything* to be normal, or the way I was before. In college, I assumed that it was "normal" to have sex with people. So I did. I regret it now, of course, but it happened. What is in the past will always be in the past and no one can do anything about it.

I now have a very strong relationship with God. He has given me everything I've always wanted and more. When I returned to high school, I was crowned homecoming queen. With lots of home school and with the help of my guidance counselor waiving some classes, I graduated on time with my high school class. I was able to go on to a State University and graduate in under ten years (keep in mind, this was all done without a fully-functional brain). I met my husband while in college, moved down to Southern California immediately after graduation, and married him. He is the love of my life. We bought a house in a quaint area and I work as an ESL teacher, teaching English to foreigners (mostly to Koreans).

* * *

What's a little Guardian Angel by your side?? It is the most spiritual feeling one can have... ever!

"How many of us have enough trust, strength, and faith to believe that we could do the impossible". -Rachel Joy Scott

"We all have our own life to pursue, our own kind of dream to be weaving, and we all have the power to make wishes come true ,as long as we keep believing". -Louisa May Alcott

"I was always looking outside myself for the strength and confidence but it comes from within. It is there all the time". -Anna Freud

"Nurture your minds with great thoughts. To believe in the heroic makes heroes". -Benjamin Disraeli

8. THE FRIENDLY... CON MAN

When I moved to L.A. back in 1998, I really did not know the kind of people I would meet here. I'm an East Coast guy from an old fashioned family with parents married more than half a century. You know what I mean... right?

So I thought I could trust everyone I met and do business with them also. Man was I wrong.

There are so many people in this country who will lie and cheat and take advantage of you, for no reason. Especially if you're broke or desperate for an opportunity like I was. A struggling actor/comedian. You see I met this guy Dave in a telemarketing room where I worked for a few months. We were selling a tax and legal course to people around the country. Yes it was hard to make money and keep interested, especially at 7 a.m. in Korea Town. The even stranger thing is that it was owned by two Turkish guys that I never knew. Yes, that happens often. We Turks get around the world.

Anyway, we became friends, so I thought, and hanging around with him going to bars and talking about potential business opportunities. That's when I ran into trouble, business opportunities. It was when we talked about how much it would cost to get things going for a real estate marketing idea we had. About $1,000 dollars. He had no money, which is why he lived with his grandparents in a beautiful house in the Hills overlooking the valley of Los Angeles. So I went there in my beat up 1997 240 SX SE and have a few drinks, watch TV and think about making money. Speaking of which, he needed a $1,000 to get him out of debt, help his girlfriend that he was crazy about and was just depressed. So being the soft hearted soul I was and still am, I had some extra money from some previous work and gave it to him. Big mistake. Huge. But the story gets better.

I was there with a few of his friends having some beers. I parked my car in front of his house way up overlooking other houses also. I put on my parking brake to make sure it would not move or roll down the hill, well that's what I expected. I'm inside trying to talk him into getting my money back because he said it would be from his grandparents within a few days, it's been over two weeks. After arguing with him on paying me back, one of Dave's friends was there also and asked where my car was. I did not really know what he meant by that, so I ran outside in a panic to see… it was not there!

We looked again and finally noticed that it somehow it rolled down the hill and almost went over the mountain side. If it actually did go over, it would have fallen on a few houses, blow up into a gas bomb, and possibly injure or kill many people. I imagined nightmares of this happening and we all got basically "freaked out" as the guys I was with said… until we saw this.

I went outside to see why my car did not go over the side of the mountain. I looked around the street it was on and saw only one telephone pole. Only ONE on the whole street. As I got closer to my car I saw that the one and only pole on the entire street stopped my car from going over! Then I looked closer if there was any damage. Remember, I did not have much money, especially giving one thousand dollars to this guy. I looked very closely at the front of my car and saw something completely amazing. The car was not damaged in any way, not one single scratch. The pole that stopped it was exactly positioned in the middle of my front bumper as if someone picked it up and guided it to the exact center of my car. The chances of this happening was incredible! We are talking rolling about twenty to thirty feet… slowly… and just stopping at the perfect speed and spot. If not, total chaos would have happened and I would have not had a car and even be in jail for not being cautious.

Being high up in the sky on this mountain near the clouds and sun, it was getting dusk and I was just thinking one thought.

What happened? How could it be? What are the chances of something like this sort of event? Then it hit me, it's like the Universe and Angel or some spirit knew it was going to happen and was clearly there to make sure no one got hurt. Again, I just kept thinking… how?

An hour later we had a tow truck come and get it straight on the street. My fake friend actually paid through his AAA card. I later found out it was his grandparents card. I left that night thinking how lucky I was.

I never did see that guy again and to be honest, I am very glad. He was someone that just cared about himself and was a drugged out crazy guy. I heard that he did get in trouble with the law and most likely went to jail. That's what happens.

I also would like to share that about a month later I got a call from my best friend Pete in San Diego. He asked me to make some phone calls for him part time to find real estate deals. Yes, real estate deals!

Just like I was planning with the Dave Loser guy, this time I work with a well-respected friend I know and trust for over thirty years. So I worked with Pete, and that year made $40,000! Man, that $1,000 did not hurt that much anymore. I felt rich… happy… it was great!

Oh well… good karma hits again!

* * *

Now I am thinking after all these years later…. *"What's a little faith"*?

There's a natural law if karma that vindictive people, who go out of there way to hurt others, will end up broke and alone. -Sylvester Stallone

Believe in yourself! Have faith in your abilities! Without a humble but reasonable confidence in your own powers you cannot be successful or happy. - Norman Vincent Peale

Optimism is the faith that leads to achievement. Nothing can be done with out hope and confidence. -Helen Keller.

How people treat you is their Karma, how you react is theirs. -Dr. Wayne Dyer.

9. MY HEAVENLY DOG

I am a huge animal lover and protect their rights any chance I get. Especially dogs and cats. So when I rescued my last two dogs from the great no-kill shelter "Pet Orphans" in Los Angeles, I was extremely happy. So let me tell you what happened when I did that. Well, there is a good point and bad point. Let's start with the bad.

When I was living with my girlfriend at the time, she kept telling me that we should get a dog. Not any dog... but a rescue dog. Now I never had a dog when I was a kid because my mother would make a big deal if I did not feed it correctly or make sure that it did not poop in the house. Mom would literally go insane if any animal made a mess in her house, especially a dog that I had promised to take care of. So when I was asked by my girlfriend to buy a dog from the rescue shelter, I said that I did not want the responsibility.

She kept after me and nagged and verbally pushed and just went on and on and on until I gave in. I said okay, let's see what we come up with. We went to so many shelters and kennels looking for that sweet little creature that would bring the most ultimate joy to our lives. We did not know what breed or color or anything really, we just wanted a freaking dog! So as a few weeks went by we finally found one. We had to make sure that he was not a barker, liked cats, and was not crazy in any way. We lived in a condo and we owned a cat. His name was Dante. Okay... we named him that because the shelter did not really have a name for him. So we went online and Googled certain dog names until we found one that was kind of different and cool.

After we took him home we thought he would be the great, mellow and sweet dog we expected. You know, just wag his tail and never bark, bite or try to run away. Man, were we wrong!

Within a few weeks of getting this monster canine, he did all of the things that we did not expect. He would run around the condo and jump on the furniture. When I took him out and forgot to put a leash on him he knew it. He would look around and see if I was paying attention to him and if I did not, he would bolt down the busy street at 20 mph. This happened many times. Once was when Dante ran down a traffic ridden street in the middle of 5 o' clock traffic. Cars would swerve around this dog while I was running top speed trying to catch him so he would not get hit and die. Yes he was a pain to take care of, but he still was my dog. I finally brought him back home and he just sat on the couch like nothing happened. Typical dog right?

Well as a few months went by, and the relationship between my girlfriend and I was coming to an end. We were together about four years and just had a different take on our future. So she moved out and wanted to take Dante with her. Well I said not so fast! I paid for him and took care of him with vet bills and other expenses. So she agreed and we shared the dog until she physically moved out. When I asked for Dante to come back to me from my ex, she would not give him back! I had a lot of problems with her and just could not get her to bring him back to his actual father.

We finally had to go to court over this. A month later I pleaded my case and she pleaded hers. I showed receipts and everything that I owned the dog and paid for all expenses. She said her name was on the license and that it was half hers. Okay technically it was. So as she was explaining to the judge why she needed that dog, it all ended up making sense to me. My ex moved in with her sister. Her older sister had a handicapped son and she took care of her. The son loved to have Dante around and be next to him. He would make him feel better and loved. I was very angry that I was not getting Dante back because I thought it was just a way for my ex to get back at me.

Then I was thinking about how that dog helped her sister's son feel better. To be loved. To have him jump all over him and basically lick him for hours at a time. I saw this young 13 year old boy and knew she was not telling the truth about this. So being the man with a soft heart, I just told the judge to let her have my canine son. He smiled at me and then at her and said "Court Dismissed."

I was with my friend at the time and she said to just let it be and get another canine friend, so I did. I went to the same shelter where I found Dante. I did look at other places before, but they all knew me there from "Pet Orphans" and said if I ever had to get another dog to come back there first.

It was very hot August day in 2007. August 21st to be exact. I went to Pet Orphans and looked at all of the cute and adorable dogs there that needed to be rescued. I looked at Dalmatians, Terriers, Pit Bulls and just about any breed you can think of. To be honest I love dogs so much, I would have taken all of them if I had a very large house. Someday I know I will. They had cats there too, which I never knew. So they took the dog I was considering who was two years old (Rocky, named after my favorite movie) and put him in a small area with cats to see if he would get along with them. He did and with no behavior issues at all. I had to do that because I also own a cat called Kismet (Turkish/Arabic for Fate) wanted to be sure that Rocky would get along with her. They do and always have. Okay… he gets jealous of her when she hangs all over me and purrs. Kismet actually does that more often when she wants something like food. Kind of like a woman to a man when she wants money for shopping. Alright, just kidding!

So I brought Rocky home and tried to get used to him being with me instead of Dante. He was okay except that he never wanted to play ball/fetch, or any kind of those games. I also attempted to play tug-of-war with a rope. He just looked at me with those sad eyes surrounded by a natural black mascara saying "no way Daddy". I just was not used to this mellow attitude. I wanted a dog to run and play and be aggressive and cocky and do all of those things that Dante did. Then as time went on, weeks and month after month I got used to his amazing love and sweetness. Whenever I walked anywhere in my home, he followed. When I went to my bed, he would jump next to me and give me huge sloppy licks. When I got ready to leave he would make sure he whimpered and made me feel guilty that I did not invite him. When I do (which is all of the time, every single place I go as long as it's good for him) he loves it. He will sit in the passenger seat and stare at me the entire time. It's almost like him saying "Thanks for saving me Papa, I love you so much and I am so happy!"

Well it's been this way for six years now. I never knew I would love an animal as much as I love my Rocky. Every morning I wake to him staring at me from a nice long sleep. He gets in this goofy mood and jumps on my neck and chest. I then pick him up and stare at his Cleopatra eyes and say "Did you sleep good?" Then I cradle him in my arms out of the bedroom and wait for his yawn. It's like the son I never had. Maybe that's why people from all over young and old, all nationalities and colors go out of their way to pet my "son". He just has this "look" about him that drives people crazy with love and admiration. He is also on the cover of my book, if you did not know.

So I wanted to share this with you. Whenever you think that a situation did not work out with a person or pet, it's for a reason. It is supposed to be that way. That's kismet, not my cat, the world's fate. It was meant to be, there is a higher order!. As the old saying says, "God closes one door and opens another". I gave Dante to my ex so he would make the handicapped boy feel better every day. I could have fought it… but again everything happens for a reason. Usually a very, very good reason.

Out of the millions of dogs in this world that needed to be rescued, I was blessed to find this one. The sweet one. The one with the mascara eyes. The dog I can't live without.

It's not a dog… it's GOD… spelled backwards! If that's what you want to believe.

Hundreds of years later, they still are important in our lives.

* * *

What's a little pet companionship? It's everything!

God bless our four legged friends!.

"Animals are such agreeable friends - they ask no questions; they pass no criticisms". -George Eliot

"The better I get to know men, the more I find myself loving dogs". -Charles de Gaulle

"The average dog is a nicer person than the average person." -Andy Rooney

"A dog is the only thing on earth that loves you more than you love yourself." - Josh Billings

10. ROY AND THE PHONE BOY

For years people always asked me how I became a telemarketer? I have been doing it for most of my life and making a great living at it since I was twenty years old. I was basically myself, but in a different character.

It all started when I did not know what the heck I was going to do for a living. I went for just two years to Ithaca College and then Monroe Community College in Rochester, NY, but did not really like it. I just like making money, plain and simple. I also really enjoy selling to people, anything at anytime, so telemarketing seemed like the way to go. I can pick up the phone and be anyone I want. One time I looked in the paper and saw an ad to work for the Monroe County Sheriffs. I said What? The Sheriffs department needs people to help raise money for them, but how?

As I interviewed for the job, I noticed it was located in the basement of a very nice office building in downtown Rochester. Yes, the basement. So I was already a little skeptical working in a dingy old basement from the 1940's and how police, fire and sheriff departments raise money to help them. It is sometimes done by selling advertisements to small and large businesses in a flashy program brochure that is given out to a vaudeville type show. The people in the show were not that popular, but still had a name. Though it was really acts that no one cared about or past its prime. They just needed the money and liked to perform. I don't want to mention names, but even if I did you would say... who?

This company was called Roy Radin Productions. They would hire local telemarketers to cold call businesses to advertise and place their company in this book for up to $2,000 at a time. Sometimes $100, $500, it depended on who you were talking to and how much they liked to help out.

Once in a while the company would come back every six months to a year and call the same companies that gave to give again. They would do this all around the country every year, all year long. It was big thing in the 1970's and 1980's. They would bring in 20K a week or more. We would say "It's that time of year again Frank, come on!" If they had an excuse and say they had to ask their wife I would say "Frank, who wears the pants in the family huh"? Or… "just take it out of your liquor money Frank, ha ha ha". It was pretty funny and it always worked. Oh, I also tried to sound like a middle aged cop called John Parker by lowering my voice, and I was twenty years old! We then had collectors drive around and pick up the checks to make sure that they would actually donate to us. Remember, no Internet or Pay Pal back then. You could also trust people more. If they said they would give money, they did. Especially if it was for the Sheriff's department. They would also get a nice decal to put on their car saying they helped. No one messed with the Sheriffs!

So one day the big man Roy Radin came by the office and stayed a few days. He would listen to the way we talked and wrote deals. The guys I worked with were like characters in a movie. One talked like the God Father, but from Boston. His phone name was Danny Athens. Some Greek guy I guess. Another was a geeky nerd guy who talked like Barney from the Andy Griffith show. I would laugh all day. There were many others also.

The week Roy was there. I wrote some pretty nice deals and was about to make $360. Now that was a lot of money to me back then, especially at twenty years old.. I lived with my parents and had no bills, I was so excited and so were my parents. Then tragedy hit. Mr. Radin saw I did not fill out the orders correctly and wanted to set an example to the rest of the guys in the office.

He had the Manager Athens cut my pay in half so I would learn a lesson, and to follow company policy. Yes… they cut my pay in half! When I saw that, I was devastated, but what was I to do? I was just a kid compared to this multi-millionaire who apparently was full of greed.

Then the next day we all went to the local bar next door. I was there looking at this large overweight man about 300 pounds 6'2 and who was worth millions. He supposedly helped the police and other organizations with raising money for them, but was actually keeping 70%! Yes, the police and Sheriffs were happy because they still made money at 30% as opposed to not making anything. It just could have been a better share.

As we were getting a little drunk, I asked Roy what it was like to run this business. Even back then I always wanted to know how to make money and how others got rich. He looked at me with a cocky look and said that he was making a tremendous amount of money and that no one should mess with him because he was bigger than… GOD!

I looked in sheer horror, and really did not know how someone could have the guts to say that. I was just stunned! I was also scared.

That comment always stuck in my mind. Kind of how John Lennon said the Beatles were more popular than Jesus. Even though Lennon did not mean it in a bad way, it came across like that. This may have been the same attitude, but seemed worse. I quit working for that company after it left Rochester and never went back.

A few years later I read in the paper that Mr. Radin was trying to raise money for a movie called the "Cotton Club". He was doing this trying to sell cocaine and other drugs, but ended doing it with the wise guys of New York at the time, if you know what I mean. It's just like what happened in that great movie "Goodfellas".

What I truly believe why this happened to him is exactly proportioned to what he said to me at the bar. He was bigger than the Lord.

Radin was kidnapped and killed on that deal that went wrong. He was only 33!

Now he did have some good points to him. He did raise money for these causes and helped thousands of officers and their families with money if they got hurt or killed in the line of duty. Bless him for that.

He did employ many around the country who made thousands a week, even back then. They also traveled the country. You may have read this in the news back in 1983, it was a very big story, but I was there. I lived to see this person. This was 100% true on seeing his character.

 One of the main things I learned in life is to watch what you think and say. It affects everyone around you.

 Be nice, not greedy. Have compassion. Treat others with respect. Don't think you are better than others, especially if you make more money than them. Money does not make you a better person. It's what you do with the money that counts. Ask other very successful people that, and they will agree.

* * *

What's a little greed?" Apparently a lot of problems when it affects others in this world!

"Making money doesn't oblige people to forfeit their honor or their conscience." - Baron Guy de Rothschild

"Let not the tie be mercenary, though the service is measured in money. Make yourself necessary to somebody. Do not make life hard to any." -Ralph Waldo Emerson

"Happiness is not in the mere possession of money; it lies in the joy of achievement, in the thrill of creative effort." -Franklin D Roosevelt

"The deepest... dream is not the hunger for money or fame; it is the dream of settling down, in peace and freedom and cooperation." -Scott Russell Saunders

11. THE MOTHER'S DECISION

A Personal Story By Shannon Reagan

November 7th, 2008; it was a beautiful morning and the third stop on our eight day long cruise through the Mexican Rivera. My two sweet kids and I were about to head out into Cabo San Lucas. My daughter Taya was really excited because it was her 11th birthday and the last port of the cruise. We got ready as fast as we could, because it was also the shortest stop. We didn't want to waste any time.

As we got off the ship, we were greeted by the usual sing of port and natives wearing traditional clothes and garb. We quickly looked around for an excursion to go on. We found a glass bottom boat ride to take us around and eventually drop us off on lover's beach for some relaxation, swimming and sightseeing. I was amazed at the sight of the famous Lands End arch, my kids were more taken with the sea life. After about a 45 minute tour, we were dropped off at Lover's beach, an amazing beach on the sea of Cortez with passage to the other side with the Pacific Ocean.

We were having a great time but I was a little nervous as my five year old son Noam was just learning to swim. I decided I wanted to walk over to the Pacific Ocean side to see the difference in sand, water, view etc. As I suspected it was incredibly magnificent. I noticed however the waves were huge and inconsistent, and the undertow was insane. We ended up running into another family from our cruise whose kids made friends with mine.

I was videotaping them at the time and had told them to stay out of the water because it looked dangerous. Just as I was asking the kids to say where they were for the camera, I noticed behind them two waves had merged creating a giant wave headed straight for them on dry land. I shouted "Run" but they thought I was playing. I suppose because they just laughed, then I pointed and started running toward them but it was too late, the wave had knocked down both my kids and one of their friends.

My daughter and the other boy were okay and being helped up by his dad, but I could not see my son. I frantically started shouting his name when suddenly I could see a piece of his arm, and his emerging look from the water with sheer terror .Oh my God... he was being dragged out to sea!

I grabbed his arm as fast as I could, but with a 45 pound backpack on and now soaking wet, I too was having trouble getting up. I was screaming for help but no one came. A woman looked on in shock but didn't move. I began digging my knees into the sand trying not to get swallowed by the sea or lose my son.

I looked up at my daughter as she looked on in horror. I was losing my grip on my son and the fight to dig into the sand to keep my position. I looked at my son and then at my daughter, and for that brief moment I had to choose and make the most important position in my life. Do I let go of my son and stay for my daughter while we possibly watch him drown to death? Or do I let go of the sand and leave my daughter alone on a beach in Mexico to watch her brother and mother die on her birthday? Then that way my son won't have to die alone. That moment felt like an eternity!

I had decided that no one was going to die, and I began using all of my god given strength and pull my son when suddenly the father of the other boy came down to help. He grabbed my son's other arm and managed to pull us both to safety. After that, I held onto both my kids and just cried - which appeared to make my son more upset, until I pulled myself together and said "okay it happened, it's over". "Everyone is still alive, let's enjoy the rest of our day" And we did. We had a lovely lunch to celebrate Taya's Birthday, then we got to hold and play with a baby tiger which was just incredible.

We talked about how that moving moment made the scary part of the day seem to disappear.

Later that night back in our room, the kids and I were watching TV, Noam had fallen asleep. I was stroking his little angelic face and

I said to Taya "We almost lost your brother today" she began to sob and say "I almost lost you both". I hugged her and we both cried and thanked God that wasn't the outcome. I will never forget the look on Noam's face as the wave had him in it's clutches. Nor will I ever forget my daughter's face as I contemplated what to do. To this day it will always remind me how much I love my children, and how I will always fight for them no matter what the cost, and how life is short.

Life can be ripped away from you at the blink of an eye, a second, as fast as a flash of light. So the message I would like to share is this:

Live each day as though there were just a few days left. We still remain friends with the man who helped us and I will always be grateful.

* * *

What's a little life without children? To the parents of the world...it is absolutely everything they live for.

"The natural state of motherhood is unselfishness. When you become a mother, you are no longer the center of your own universe. You relinquish that position to your children" -Jessica Lange

"When you are a mother, you are never really alone in your thoughts. A mother always has to think twice, once for herself and once for her child." -Sophia Loren

I loved raising my kids. I loved the process ,the dirt of it, the tears of it, the frustration of it, Christmas, Easter, birthdays, growth charts, pediatrician appointments. I loved all of it. -Jane Elliot

12. THINK… SEE… AND BELIEVE

Millions of people over the last 50 years or more have heard many of the great leaders in motivation and positive thinking say this one thing "You are what you think". Dr. Wayne Dyer, Anthony Robbins, Less Brown and many more. Well I can say that is so true, but it's also what you see and sometimes look like or portray. This is especially true in theater and TV/Film. I know, because I have heard many of the same things about my "look" over and over again. Was I a boxer? A wrestler? Fighter? Cop? Mechanic? And the best one, a Mafia guy like from the Sopranos. Seriously, I have heard it all.

Sometimes, I would get upset and say no...I am none of those things. Leave me alone! Then other times I would laugh it off. I was wondering about how type-casting worked in Hollywood. I thought that it would be a bad thing in your career to let that happen. I mean who wants to play the same part over and over again. I'm a comedian sitcom guy. Well in the industry of make believe, it can be a good thing. Make a living at how people see you and you see yourself.

Well, being here in Los Angeles for 15 years and trying to make it, I decided to see if that type-casting formula worked for me. Once I made that decision to accept my look and the thinking behind it, everything came together. So I decided to get some photos of me as these so called characters/people everyone has been calling me. I did the cop and all that, even the Mafia-gangster type. So I decided to market myself like that to the casting directors, agents and managers. Within a few weeks of doing that, I got the call that was the type I have been waiting for all my life. The "call" that just made sense and something I could be proud of and talk about to friends and family until the day I passed on.

I am at my home and get a call from Central Casting. They were looking for a Mafia type guy for a huge feature film that Warner Brothers was making. I asked a few questions and all I heard is that the producers wanted me to be in the film. I said... "you sure it's me"? Yes the guy said. So I went to the audition, even though I was sure I am in the movie. There were eight others there all dressed up like the Godfather days. The main person in charge of casting on the set looked at the others, then me. He knew me from looking at my pictures for about a week. Then the producer came over and gave us the "eye". He was the final person in selecting us. So after that, we got to go home. Oh... after we got paid that is. That's the great thing about the Screen Actors Union. You get PAID to do things like auditions and wardrobe.

The next morning I called to see if I really was in the movie. I could not wait for them to call me in the afternoon. I made it...it happened! I ended up with four other guys on the set, but I worked the most on camera. Not only did I work on camera, I was next to the biggest film icons in Hollywood history.

You see, it was not just a movie. It was a potential Blockbuster that will come out in June 2014. It had stars and huge great top ten songs in there also. The movie that I got cast in was something I have been thinking about for a few years. I sang the songs and even did impressions of the icons I just mentioned. The Hollywood legends I spent three days with and felt like I was in a dream world were Clint Eastwood and Christopher Walken. The movie was "Jersey Boys" Clint directed while Christopher was the star. I was the guy who protected Walken's character Gyb. Here I am in this movie with 30 people looking at me on the set. The Mafia guy. The guy that I did not want to be all my life, but now am...and love it.

The strangest thing is that I have been doing impressions of Clint Eastwood since the 1970's with "Well Punk did I fire five shots or six"? and 1980s with "Go ahead...make my day". Now he is next to me while saying "Hi Jon, how's it going:? I wanted to say "Great Punk" but almost fainted. Chris Walken said, "You know, you make a good tough guy". I said, "Thank you boss." Then I pinched myself.

Not only was I doing impressions of them in my stand-up act for years, I also sang certain songs that I love in my Karaoke act. One of the songs I did was "Big girls don't cry" by Franki Valli and the 4 Seasons. I did his voice and mannerisms so well along with some other songs, that it almost landed me a spot on "Americas Got Talent" on NBC!

But that's what "Jersey Boys" is about. The life and times of how Franki Valli got started over 50 years ago and is now a major Broadway play the past five years. I thought it into my life! See what I mean? Franki never gave up… I did not either.

So when you "think" about what you want in life, go for it. Then "look" the part as if you are what you want in life, it happens. Trust me. Ask Stallone when he made "Rocky." also. You know his story. It's like a vision board of life.

* * *

What's a little positive thinking and belief? It means everything!!

"No matter what your going through, there's a light at the end of the tunnel and it may seem hard to get to it, but you can do it and just keep working towards it and you'll find the positive side of things." -Demi Lovato

"If you have a positive attitude and constantly strive to give your best effort, eventually you will overcome your immediate problems and find you are ready for greater challenges." -Pat Riley

"Winners make a habit of manufacturing their own positive expectations in advance of the event" -Brian Tracy

13. THE X MAN ROOMMATE

I was in Miami, Florida talking to others about coming to Los Angeles to pursue my acting career. Many of my friends said they knew people who went there and were going to stay...but did not. They didn't have friends there, could not meet the right people (also known as connections) or what I have heard countless times, ran out of money. That's not good.

Well after hearing these stories and being the pushy positive person I am, I said that I will try the LA scene myself. One of the interesting things that happened is just when I was thinking about that, I was editing my acting reel to take to LA with me. I did not really know what I was doing on how the scenes should look like, how long the contents should be, etc. My editors did not know the creative aspect, but this one guy who happened to be there did. His name was Xavier. We called him X, like X-Men, Malcolm X, you get it. I guess it's a Cuban religious name is what I heard.

He was looking at what was shot and said to cut here, change that and so on. We also got along and laughed at the same things, then found out he was an actor and producer. He also lived in LA a few years before that in the 1990's, but came back to Miami for some personal reasons. I later found out that the X guy wanted to move back to LA, and soon. So we both decided to move out together and be roommates. I thought it was a great idea since he lived there before, actually produced movies, and was an actor with credits. Big credits like Miami Vice with Don Johnson, General Hospital, and other films. He would give me advice and turn me on to his friends and "Connections" he had.

So a few weeks later I left, and a few weeks later after that X man came. Now I really don't like to live with roommates, especially someone I just met. I thought, what the heck, I would give it a try. I later found out that it was a big mistake and will explain why.

It all started going to our first Halloween party on Sunset Blvd. We got dressed up like the Blues Brothers. He played the Belushi character and I of course was Dan Aykroyd. The time was great and we met so many cool people. It was like that over the months of going out. Like getting into clubs where you had to "know" someone. I would also go to screenings of movies, industry parties with actors from top shows and others that produce and direct. Some of these Hollywood parties that I went to got pretty crazy with the drinks, drugs and weird situations. Remember its LA, not Cleveland or Rochester, NY. This was strange to me. I am just a regular East coast guy that come from old fashioned Turkish parents. I am also nice and basically will talk to anyone, anytime, I don't care. Most people I met only talk with you if you can help them. That's it. So sad.

As time went on the X man would introduce me to more people in LA along with more insane parties. The thing I did not know was how strong and good looking he was when he was ten to fifteen years younger. He showed me photos. and I did not even recognize him. He was forty pounds thinner and exercised all the time riding his bike 10 miles a week. This was amazing to me. He was a ladies man and was very popular in the social circles. I was jealous. Then all this changed after I was his friend.

What happened is he went though some personal and family issues. His parents divorced and then he lost his mom, got in a motorcycle accident and almost died. X was not that close to his Cuban father and brothers either. I was shocked to hear all these stories.

I was always there to help him in any way. He borrowed money from me to pay his bills and of course rent. I actually bought him a used car to get back and forth to work and other parts of LA. You just can't live without a car in LA.

We tried to start a production company and a group of film makers called "Event United," but it went nowhere. Things just started to go downhill for us, especially him. This is what happened... drugs and alcohol. Yes, so common these days, actually it's been that common for over many decades.

He would have his drinks, pot, a pack of cigarettes a day, and other substances that was just going out of control. We had friends tell him to stop. His old girlfriends would say that too. Even his family, but no deal. I did have him take a break from all that and exercise more by running around the track at the local park. That lasted about...two days. I liked him so much because when he was not under the influence, he was funny and polite, and just a great person. X would even talk with my mom and brothers on the phone. He was also spiritual and a strong believer in the "man upstairs" is how he put it. We even went to the famous "Little Brown Church" in Studio City which is part of Los Angeles. He would have me sit still and watch him kneel and pray for guidance and forgiveness. This little church looks like a small one bedroom house and is open 24/7.

It is for anyone at any time young, old, white, black, poor or rich. It just did not matter. I thought that I was lucky to have him in my life... but only when he was clean and sober.

After being his roommate and friend for a few years I just could not take it anymore, I had to leave. The minute I did, my life got better and less stressful. I started making great money, got my Real Estate license, dated some amazing girlfriends, I was just so happy. Oh ,not only was I his roommate in our first apartment, we lived in two other apartment's also. We moved three times in two years! I was his roommate and a very good friend. It just did not help him.

Many years later I asked a good friend who knew the X man and wanted to see what happened to him. Did he move back to Miami? Was he acting and producing? Was he okay? None of the above. I was sad to hear he passed away in Miami. I'm not sure how it happened, but I heard that it was his failing health. I was heart-broken to hear that, but not too surprised. Yes we had our differences and got very hard to live with him, or anyone really. It's just when you don't take care of yourself, you hurt others around you that don't want the health issues to affect your relationship. Whether it's a husband and wife, brother and sister, any relative and of course roommates. Two things I learned over the years and found out it's extremely important is this "You are who you associate with!". Whether it's personal or business. Also, "Health is Wealth!" The last one came from my sweet Mom.

My mother would say in Turkish, and of course her thick Turkish accent. "Jon...someone could have a million dollars in the bank, but if they don't stay healthy, it just does not matter". One thing I always remembered was my mom yelling at me when I was a kid. "Jon... Drink your milk!" "Don't eat too much!" That's Mom for yah. Thanks Mom.

So use this as your guide to life. It's not just the money and big cars and all the materialistic things in life… it's YOUR HEALTH!

Family and friends of course, but you have to live long enough to enjoy them.

* * *

So what's a Little Health? It's everything you should live for!.

"Health, learning and virtue will ensure your happiness; they will give you a quiet conscience, private esteem and public honor." -Thomas Jefferson

"Friendship, love, health, energy, enthusiasm, and joy are the things that make life worth living and exploring." -Denise Austin

"A man too busy to take care of his health is like a mechanic too busy to take care of his tools." -Spanish Proverb

14. "HE'S GOOD PEOPLE"

One of the best sales positions I had as a telemarketer was when I lived in North Miami Beach, Florida in 1997. I did not know if I wanted to stay in Florida or pursue my dreams of being a working actor in Los Angeles.

I was leaning towards moving until I looked at my bank account and almost cried. Okay… maybe not that bad, but it was pretty sad compared to my other friends making 80k a year or more in sales and other companies they started. So I stayed. I first started working at a very well known time share company and setting up appointments for tourists to come and visit the resort. When they did come, I got paid. But as usual not enough. The people I worked with were very nice, but I knew I was not going anywhere. So a friend of mine that got fired from there went down the hall to another company he heard about and knew others working there. So I decided to check it out.

I found out that it was a company that helped people win money playing the Florida Lottery. Yes the Lottery done over the phone around the country. We would have openers call people off a list who like playing the lottery, Bingo, race horses, basically anything that deals with gambling. Then we would have them play a small game for about $10. I would call them back the next day and get them to play another game for more money, but better odds of winning more also. I would also ask for hundreds or thousands at a time and have them charge it on their credit card.

I would talk to the most strangest people in the world. Farmers, business owners, married couples, gay couples, students, you name it, I heard it. I also would work with weird people in the office. You know the kind you see in movies and TV shows, but they really do exist. I am sure others have worked with these types also. The druggies, the sleazy girls, even the nerds. I did have a funny manager that was in charge called Lenny. This guy was a walking joke machine like Rodney Dangerfield on speed. It was one liner after another, and most of them were not that funny...but he was trying to be. When the sales people made deals, they would go to this huge white board and write them down. The total was done every day. I was always the top seller...always!. So you know what happens when you start making money for people like the guys I worked for? You become "Good People".

As the months went on, brand new management took over. Lenny moved on to another job, and some guys from NY came in to...you know.. "Keep an eye on things, and show respect, know what I mean?". So after working there, I would see these guys come in to watch us work. There was "Fat Tony" who just sat around and listened to us talk and not say the wrong things that could get us busted and in jail. Fat Tony was 350 pounds. When he talked it sounded like he was gargling sand paper and gravel. Then we had his boss fat, but slimmer Jimmy. He was always paranoid and would go up to me and explain what's going on. I asked why people are coming and going. He did not know the term behind this, so I just looked at him straight in his eyes and said "Oh… we are going through a transition period, right?" He then thought about it for about ten seconds, looked at the ceiling then me and screamed in his Brooklyn accent "YEAH… THATS IT!"

Other times guys would come in and ask for me, but would butcher my name. There would be four or five older guys in their 60's and 70s who wore pink shirts and green pants smoking very huge cigars. Expensive Cuban cigars that cost 20 bucks each. They looked like they just came off the set of "Goodfellas". They would say "Hey where's that Parcheesi, Princki, Paraneechi". One time a guy called Vinnie was so tired and lazy he called me Pacino. Yes, like AL.

As time went on they kept on calling me "Good People" cause I was making them thousands a week in profit. I was doing great too. Boo

Coo bucks as we would say sometimes.

They would also take me and the other "boys" out to dinner and watch me perform stand up comedy while they ate their antipasto and gnocchi with grated cheese. I would go out with them a few times a week and they would pay for everything. God forbid I tried to even pay the tip. One of the guys called "Lazy Louie" would say "Hey… Forget about it! What are you trying to embarrass me in front of my people?" I never tried to pay again so I didn't get whacked! Okay… maybe not that, but get them angry.

I became friends with them and they would always compliment me and the voices-impressions I did. Some were the other guys like "Fat Jimmy," they loved that one! They kept on saying.." Hey Pirincki… I mean Pirincci… Jonny, you need to get out of here!" I said what? "You need to do Vegas or Hollywood, you know what I mean?" I had a real good guy Sal who did the accounting for us with another Jewish guy Barry. Sal told me to take a trip to New York city and do some clubs there first. He said to go through the Bronx and have dinner at his friends Vinnie's restaurant and he would take care of me. It was like I was going to eat at a small Italian Restaurant like in the first Godfather film where Michael shoots the corrupt cop. No charge! Just tell him Sal sent you from Miami. So every night after work and eating the best pasta places Miami had to offer, I would come home and think… maybe they are right. Maybe I should follow my dreams!

As time went on a few more months, I found out that the office was closing down. The big boys went on to bigger and better deals. We ended up to be "small time, peanuts" for them. It was now September 1998. My other friends were getting married, I had no girlfriend, no cool guys to hit Ft Lauderdale or any other clubs like the old days a few years ago. The great thing now is that I had money...a lot of it.

So I picked a date… September 14th. I shipped my car out to LA, a week later I followed. I made it… I was here. I listened to "the boys" and my "good people". I was home. I did what other successful people have done, I followed my gut and intuition. The worst thing that could happen is I get to live In LA with the movie and TV stars. I just had to do it, if not, I would regret it the rest of my life.

Everyone should think and do the same. No matter who you are and what you do in life now.

* * *

So when you think about what happened... *What's a little faith and good friends?*

Believe in your talent, a lot. Always, always follow your dreams and be around others that will believe in you... if not... like my Italian friends said my whole life... FORGET ABOUT IT!!

"Just don't give up trying to do what you really want to do. Where there's love and inspiration, I don't think you can go wrong". -Ella Jane Fitzgerald

"Visualize this thing you want. See it, feel it, believe in it. Make your mental blueprint and begin." -Robert Collier

"Ambition is the path to success. Persistence is the vehicle you arrive in" -Bill Bradley

"Unless commitment is made, there are only promises and hopes... but no plans" -Paul F. Drucker

15. THE NO-HOME MAN

One day I was very upset with my life. Ever have one of those days where you think "What on earth am I doing here? What is my purpose? You just feel like not waking up and if you do, you just want to watch TV and eat cupcakes and chocolate ice cream. Yes, even a few donuts. Well that is how I was that sunny morning in July 2013. It was a Wednesday afternoon about 1 pm and I was off to work at a new job. A job I was not excited about and hesitated to even drive there, which was only 10 minutes away.

I was hired to sell theater tickets to many shows here in Los Angeles. I thought it was going to be easy. I give them discounts to subscriptions so they can see new shows they never saw before. The problem was, I would call and 90% of the time get a voice mail at their home and cell. Man, it was irritating. Okay I got paid 10 bucks an hour, but the deal was to make a commission on each sale! That would add to a very good paycheck. Yeah right, I will make more money talking to no one. Every ten minutes I went to the water cooler and then grab another doughnut. Another ten minutes, more water and 2 more donuts. I was going insane!!

So when I got my break I walked across the street, to just get some air. Then I was thinking about how I was going to leave this job, but still pay the rent. I was absolutely miserable. What do I do? My life sucked! Then "The Man" showed up. Yes... the "Man." I was waiting outside near my car and thinking of getting lunch. Can I afford lunch? Okay, maybe a special deal at Subway or Burger King for under 5 bucks, that's all I could afford. As I contemplated my hunger and life in general, I looked over to my hard left and saw through my sunglasses a tired man.

He was about 60 years old and had the typical look of a sad depressed homeless man. He was carrying a bag and had torn jeans, beat up shoes, heavy jacket in 80 degree weather, a filthy beard and just looked terrible. When I looked at him, I saw just a touch of me also. Maybe not in a physical sense, but mentally anguished inside. I kept looking at him and did not know what to do. Do I just ignore him like the other men that walked by him in their $500 suits? Then the women were staring at him wondering how this man got this way, why is he there? While they walked in their $600 Jimmy Choo shoes!

Then it finally hit me. I just was wondering how really bad I do not have it. All these memories came to me about my mom saying I should help others. That it's not about money and materialistic possessions. It's not about that at all.

It's about Health, Family, Friends, a higher spirit and helping others.

So as these feelings were hitting me, I walked up to that "man" and looked into his sad eyes glazed over with no future. I waited for him to sit down near the corner of the office building he just walked to. As he got a little settled on the sidewalk, I went to him and said "Hi, how's it going? He just looked at me. I said "Are you okay"? He just stared at me again and had a small little mumble, almost like he could not speak at all. Normally from others that are like that, they can at least say a few words, his was nothing.

So I reached in my pocket and pulled out what little money I had at the time, about five dollars. I gave it to him as he looked at me and thinking "Why is he doing this"? "He does not have to help me." I said please use it to buy food or anything else you need. He stared at me again and just nodded and mumbled... okay.

Now here is what happened to me, which normally it does not that often. As I walked away I went to the corner of the sidewalk and hesitated. I was thinking to myself, "What in the heck am I complaining about? Look at him and look at me. I am a fool!" All of a sudden an amazing rush of emotion hit me... and I started to cry. Yeah... a grown man in his 50's in the middle of a sunny work day... crying. I could not help it. It's almost like the world of Karma said

"Shame on you Jon for complaining." But it also explained how much it meant to me about helping this person. Even though it was not that much, but just the act of giving made me feel so good. Dr. Wayne Dyer once said that endorphins attack the system of affection when people do that. Even if it's a quarter... it's the same as giving a hundred dollars!

So after that I composed myself and went back to my work. I did not feel the same after that, and when I went back home I called my mother and told her what happened. She said that by helping others like I did, it would come back to me in many good ways. That is why I am healthy and always make a decent living to afford a car, apartment and many other things that the "man" and many more do not have.

I now help others all the time when it comes to this. A few dollars here, a few dollars there. Women holding a child with a sign saying that she is homeless. The man on the ground in front of a store. The toothless old man on the side of the highway.

Every time I do help, something always better happens to me...always!. Try it and you will see. Trust me...it works.

* * *

What's a little compassion? It's everything that makes the world just a better place!

"Let us touch the dying, the poor, the lonely and the unwanted according to the graces we have received and let us not be ashamed or slow to do the humble work." -Mother Teresa

"To love means loving the unlovable. To forgive means pardoning the unpardonable. Faith means believing the unbelievable. Hope means hoping when everything seems hopeless." -G.K Chesterton

"Life has never been easy. Nor is it meant to be. It is a matter of being joyous in the face of sorrow" -Dirk Benedict

"The cure for sorrow is to learn something" -Barbara Sher

"There is something terribly morbid in the modern sympathy with pain. One should sympathies with the color, the beauty, the joy of life. The less said about life's sores, the better." -Oscar Wilde

"A person has sympathy for mankind in the lump, faith in its futures progress, and desire to serve the great cause of his progress, should be called not a humanist, but a humanitarian, and is creed may be designated as humanitarianism" -Irving Babbitt

16. HONESTY… FOR LIFE

One of the best things about living in Disney World… I mean Orlando Florida, are the people. Okay, not just the people, but the tourists. I had a chance to meet hundreds of them over a few years working in the time share business.

I would have booths up and down International Drive in front of stores, restaurants, hotels, basically any place where a tourist would walk and spend their hard earned cash. So I would work these booths and set up my brochures and maps and ticket information to prove to them one thing. If they just spent 90 min of their precious time, they would save big bucks on one day passes to Disney World, Universal Studios, Sea World, Medieval Times and many other attractions. Most of these savings would be as much as 50% off and even include free dinners/drinks etc. I would explain to them that they need to set up an appointment with me, then I tell my manager. They then go at a certain time to visit the Resort. When they show up they would get a nice respectful and persuasive pitch to spend about 50-100K on this beautiful place that they would see only about one to two weeks a year. Some people never see it since they have to fly from Europe or even China and Japan, and it would just cost too much.

It was hard to understand some of the accents these humans would use when talking to just a regular guy like me from Rochester, NY. The British would be very polite and never complain about anything because if they did, it would be embarrassing to them and Mother Queen. Even if they did swear or complain and yell in a high tone of voice, their accent is so pleasant no one would care. "You know, mate, you're really a stupid person!" Well thank you. Then I had the married couples and singles from Ireland. Most of the time I could not understand them either. They would talk like the Leprechaun from Lucky Charms cereal commercials. I would look at them with my discounted tickets and do their accent. Sometimes they laughed, other times the guy would take a swing at me and then walk away. Of course they missed. Germans tried to be nice but had no sense of humor. They also all looked tall and blonde, men and women. I remember one guy was called Hans and he talked like Arnold Schwarzenegger from the Terminator. Give me the Tickets...NOW! The French sounded like Pepe LePew, the skunk from the Tiny Toons cartoon. I also could never understand that when a woman swears at someone they always try to be polite and say "Pardon my French, but your an ass…" Why not just cuss and be done with it.

I have seen and heard it all from Israelis, Persians, Turks, Armenians. Even the hard working rednecks that saved their money all year long to make it and see the famous mouse.

So I remember how busy it got in the summer time when all the Tourists came with the their families. Summer and Christmas were the most crazy times. One day I was selling some extra Disney tickets I had from a tourist that could not use the four day pass. I did that on purpose to help them out, and I also would make a few bucks to pay my bills. One time I met a very nice Chinese family that lived in Peking, China. They were here to take their kids to Disney World and all the other attractions there. I still remember what the woman was talking about while I was explaining how the time share program worked. She was so excited to be there and make her husband and mostly the kids have the time of there lives. Remember, it's a 14 hour flight! After a half an hour and going over all the details, we exchanged money for some extra Disney tickets I had and also her appointment to see the beautiful resort. Oh, I also wanted to point out that she did all the talking and negotiating with me. The husband just stood there and smiled bobbing his head up and down. I guess that's the way it is in the Asian culture. Women RULE!

So after we talked and was done with everything, I said good bye and to enjoy their vacation. I get very personal and tell them my name and where I am from also in case they want to come back for more business or had questions. As the night went on it just got busier and busier towards 10, 11 p.m., then midnight… it was crazy. You got kids dragging their parents all over, newlyweds kissing, holding hands and of course guys looking for women to get lucky.

I was just about to finish my shift and noticed I had a lot of cash. It seemed like everything was okay after I did the accounting. I was very happy but tired and ready to go home. I was saying good bye to some people I worked with and finding out where I was going the next night to work on the famous International Drive. When I was getting my papers in order, I looked up and saw a family coming towards me. I looked at them and they looked familiar from maybe that night a few hours ago. I meet so many people a night that I forget. Then I see the woman comeback and start yelling at me "Mr. Jon… MR. JON!" I got nervous on why some person was calling my name in the middle of the parking lot near my booth. Did they have a complaint? Did I forget to give them their tickets or maybe directions to the resort? No… it was neither of those. It was the Asian woman from China. She ran back to me and said that I made a mistake. A BIG Mistake. I was mistaken in giving her the wrong change when she bought my tickets. I said "Oh I'm sorry, I get busy and sometimes forget or count wrong." But that's not what happened at all. She said that when she was looking through her purse, she noticed that I gave her an extra nne hundred bill!. I immediately looked through my cash and noticed that I was short one hundred dollars. She could have used the extra hundred bucks for many things back in 1988. A nice restaurant, souvenirs for the kids, even enough to buy four Sea World tickets. But no… she did not do that. She went out of her way to come back and give that to me knowing deep down inside I really needed it.

I just looked at her in disbelief and excitement. I never had any one do that before… ever! To go out of her way to come back hours later out of sheer honesty. I remember vividly that I took the money when she gave it to me and actually grabbed and hugged her. I even kissed her on the cheek and said thank you so much for doing that. I also shook the husbands hand for being honest. Then I was thinking to myself, for just creating good Karma.

She did not seem like it was really a big deal to her. It was to me!.

She left towards her car and never saw her again. Then a few days later I was looking into other cultures compared to Americans. Yes we are nice people in this country, but when it comes to morals and being honest, we unfortunately have some work to do.

I found out in the Asian culture that people I have talked to and met told me that's the way it is there. People have left wallets on subways in Tokyo, Singapore, Beijing, Taiwan and come back hours later… and it would still be there! I actually remembered this story before and ran into a similar situation in Trader Joes in LA. I was talking with a cashier and the lady before me left her wallet with cash and credit cards, license, her whole identity. I could have stolen it, but did not. I could not live with myself if I did. The cashier gave it back to the woman and she was so happy. So was I. Since I did that nice gesture I later went back home to make some calls for business I had. On one call I made a deal that landed me a $1,000 commission. Do you see what I mean? Get it? It came back to me in a good way.

* * *

What's a little Honesty? As you can see here….everything!!

"Six essential qualities that are the key to success: sincerity, personal integrity, humility, courtesy, wisdom ,charity" -Dr. William Claire Menninger

"The roots of all goodness lie in the soil of appreciation for goodness" -the 14th Dalai Lama

"Honest towards ourselves and towards anyone else who is our friend, brave towards the enemy, magnanimous towards the defeated, polite always: This is how the four cardinal virtues want us to act. -Friedrich Nietzsche.

17. JAY AND JON... THE JAWS OF HUMOR

For as long as I can remember I have been doing voices and faces of people I know or met. When I was nine years old I had these friends who were students in my grade school Buckman Heights. It was located in Rochester, NY... Greece was the suburb.

For some reason I just had this knack to change my voice and try to sound like others. I remember this one chubby Italian guy called Sal. Most of the kids in Rochester were Italian and called either Sal, Joey, or Vinnie. This was back in the 1960's and when I go back to visit even now, it's still the same names!

Anyway, he talked in this high voice almost like a girl and the other kids made fun of him. So of course me being the potential comedian, I had to do it and make others laugh. Yes... they did laugh. There was even a girl called Kirsten. She was this hot blonde German girl we all liked. She had this crazy German accent that sounded so weird, we did not know where it came from. The others would ask if I can do that voice, so I tried. Now being nine years old, you can get pretty high on the octaves. So I did do it while thinking of a German I knew, Col Klink from "Hogan's Heroes" TV show.

For years I would be doing voices and faces from TV and films. I would always do teachers behind their back. Man I would get these crazy laughs. I know for a fact I got my humor from my Turkish mom. Why is she funny? I don't know, but she is.

As the years went by, stand-up comedy was growing in popularity. Clubs would open up all over the US because it was cheap to produce and advertise. I mean all you really needed was a microphone, a small stage and seats to watch the comics that never got paid well... even to this day.

So when all this was going on I kept thinking that I should start performing. So I did. It was at a restaurant in a plaza called the Casablanca, owned by two Greek brothers Bill and George. I would go in there and start doing open mics and then got better and better to do shows on their stage. Opening for certain bands like the Byrds and other comics like Sandra Bernhardt and Andrew Dice Clay before he changed his name to that.

One of the best influences I had from watching other comics was their material. I like to be mostly clean with my impressions. The best comics back then were Seinfeld and Leno. Especially Leno. He would just go on the stage and kill from the first minute to the last, one hour later. I had a chance to meet him back stage a few times and he would give me advice and others "to just be yourself."

Well that was easy for me. I always had this connection with Jay. Especially the way I looked, with my chin. For years people would come and say I look like Jay, except my chin is smaller. It's like a baby Leno jaw. I mean how many times can I hear this? I of course looked in the mirror and saw the resemblance. I would also talk like Jay to see if I can pull it off. I can. I just talk like I have helium in my voice, add a lisp and move my hands around like a puppet while nodding my head.

A few years later I would win a radio contest for the funniest person in Rochester. The winner gets to see Jay Leno at a show at Geneseo State college. Free tickets, a limo and the whole nine yards. So of course I won. I did Pee Wee Herman, Rocky Balboa and of course, Jay. The great thing was that when I went to see and tell him I won this contest, he remembered me from the past few times I saw him at other clubs. He went "I remember you." We talked for a few minutes and I asked him if I can introduce him to the crowd of about 3,000 people. He said sure... but wanted to know if I wanted to open the show for him and do about 5 min.

I could not believe it and of course said YES. I ended up doing a great 5 min set in front of the most people I have ever performed in front of ever. Even now, it's tough to do that unless you are Louis CK or Larry the cable guy. I did a celebrity version of Wheel of Fortune. I did Jack Nicholson, Reverend Jim Ignatowski from the sitcom Taxi, and Rocky Balboa. I now do Owen Wilson, Al Bundy, Seth Rogan and others that at I throw in from time to time. That show was so popular back then and even now..30 yrs later.

The great thing about this journey of comedy and my association with Jay is it still is there many years later. I ended up seeing him drive his Stanley Steamer car from the 1930's and said "hi." Then watch him eat at his favorite, and mine, a Fallafal outdoor restaurant. I said hi to him and again, he remembered me! A few months later I ended up being on his show in a sketch video called "The Siphon." It was a fake game show where you stole gas from other cars tanks. Very funny.

Here is where the story gets motivating to me and should be to you. When I look at certain peoples past and present, I wonder what it was like for them and for me. What are their parents like? What did they do? How did it influence the way they were raised and then the career they chose. Again I have always been told I have a chin like Jay. Smaller, but have it. My mom could never understand how… but I do. Maybe it was the mail man… just kidding Mom.

Jay's parents were old fashioned and strict, just like mine. His dad was an insurance salesman. My dad, a cardiologist. Both our moms were housewives. His dad was funny. My mom was. They supported Jay in whatever he did to make money and do comedy. My parents again did the same wth me. Yes they tried to talk me out being a comedian, but I did not listen. Leno's from the East coast, Boston, I'm NY, Rochester. He has old fashioned morals and values, so do I. His parents were married over 50 years… ditto here.

My point is this. Look at other people you admire and learn about them. Be like them. Copy them. Don't be jealous of them but listen to them. Knowledge is the key. Always take advice from others you admire and think can help you. Jay has always been that type of guy. Nice and smart with advice.

* * *

What's a little Jealousy? It can be life changing in a bad way! Don't let it affect you… ever!

Just stay the course you want in your life.

"Keep your dreams alive. Understand to achieve anything requires faith and belief in yourself, vision, hard work, determination, and dedication. Remember all things are possible for those who believe." -Gail Devers

"Winners make a habit of manufacturing their own positive expectations in advance of the event." -Brian Tracy

"Do the one thing you think you cannot do. Fail at it. Try again. Do it better the second time. The only people who never tumble are those who never mount the high wire. This is your moment. Own it." -Oprah Winfrey

"Choosing to be positive and having a grateful attitude is going to determine how your going to live your life" -Joel Osteen

18. NEIGHBORS

Ever move into a new neighborhood and get excited that you will meet new and interesting people? It could be that new house you just bought. Then again, if you are like most people in this country, maybe the world, you just rent an apartment or a house. Either way you are entering new surroundings that you never saw before.

It could be that you moved into a new city to pursue a new job or business opportunity. You could have fallen in love and wanted to be near your partner, or just your family. Whatever the case, you are going to be near different people and how they become your "new neighbor." The problem is that these days when you do actually and physically move in and want to meet your new so called friends, it does not happen. Everyone knows what this is, and have gone through it. It's called "people are scared to meet others." Not just scared, terrified, sad huh? What the heck happened to us as a society?.

I have moved to three different cities over a 25 year period. I was raised in Rochester, New York, Orlando, Florida, then Miami, and now Los Angeles. When I moved to Orlando back in 1988, I knew a few people who were friends from years ago. Yes I had fun with them, but when I went home to my apartment, I knew no one. I would walk to the pool and parts of the complex and really talked with again, no one. I had neighbors who lived right next to me, we are talking five feet to the left and right. Did not know their name, or barely what they looked like.

The same thing happened when I moved to Miami. I lived in a few houses that we invested in to repair and sell after the great Hurricane Andrew. Hardly knew any one that lived next to us. We were there for a few years, no idea who was there. They could have been aliens from Mars. I might as well live in a ghost town with those dried up tumble weeds going by like in the TV shows and movies. Gun smoke anyone?

So I decided to move into another beautiful apartment complex on the ocean in upscale Bal Harbour, Florida. I thought that again it's a new part of Miami and a little more high class. There were at least one hundred apartments in the building. That's at least a hundred new friends I could make. I was so excited to meet them. After a few months of trying, nothing. I would swim in the pool, and I was usually the only one there. Even if I wasn't, I was.

Then my life took me to Los Angeles. The city of Angels. Hollywood. Lights, Camera, Action! I was incredibly excited now. Friends galore, maybe finally find a nice girl, date her and get married. Just like my parents. Okay close, but not happening. There was that in parts of LA, but it was very hard, and still is to meet new people that live right next to me. I was so frustrated that I had to ask others that went though this. Moving and not knowing who is next to you. The shadow that moves in the window. Over 90% said, "That's just the way it is now Jon… it's just the way it is." So disappointing.

Then I was wondering about where and when I was raised. Was it like that back then? Did more people know others and made friends? You know, "Can I borrow a cup of sugar?" Well it was. That's how Rochester NY where I was raised in the 1960's and 70's was. Sort of like Mayberry where Barney and Andy knew every single person in that town. I did too… sort of.

I would go back to my home town every single year to visit my mom, brothers, family and close friends. I would go back to my same bedroom I had as a ten year old child, and see memories of my childhood. I would drive around the old neighborhood and literally remember the names of the grade school and high school friends that lived there. Every street. Every house. Every name. I even remember their parents, brothers, sisters, what sports they liked, almost anything.

We are talking well over forty years ago. My point is, that's the way it used to be back then, remember? Maybe you don't. Let me tell you the details.

Back in the 1960's - 70's people and society were different. The way they treated each other with respect and also helped each other. Kids did not get scared walking alone down the road to school. Bad things did not happen to them because everyone knew each other. All the neighbors also knew what each other did for professions. I know, because I was that kid. This ten year old kid would walk to school by himself, no other friends, just me and my books. The neighbors would wave hello to me as I walked down the road to my school. Most of them knew my dad the doctor who lived in the yellow house on the corner. For years I was known as the Doctor's son. It felt proud to be called that. Most of them would be my dad's patients too. I also knew who they were and what "they" did. I had many, many close friends and would be invited to dinner and small parties they had. The funny thing is that I knew a lot about my friends, even though they were not really "close" friends.

When we trick-or-treated on Halloween with our masks and Batman costumes on, it was again just us. Yes once in a while we had a few parents, but nothing like today. It would just be me and a few others. We never heard about kids getting taken, kidnapped or drugged. Never! I ate whatever candy I wanted, and as much as I wanted. Then I would watch the Charlie Brown Halloween special. Oh, the good ole days.

My friend Adam and I would ride our bikes to the Farm View stand to get Bazooka gum. It was only one penny!. Then go to other places for miles around on our bikes. I would know where everyone lived because to us, they were neighbors. I am talking a five to ten mile radius. Years ago, my friends' mothers would take us in the car to go shopping or soccer games. They were the real soccer moms back then.

I would also go to my friend Ray in the summertime and watch that old Disney Classic "Song of the South" in their garage with about twenty other "neighbors." Oh, to be young again.

Now, I do not know anyone in my buildings. I might get lucky and see someone that liked my dog Rocky. Oh, ever notice they will always know your dog's name, but not yours? I know, always. In the good ole days, parents would watch other parent's kids. Not just for a night, sometimes a week. If the kid was not respectful to the adults, or others, they would report them to the parents. Notice how I said parents. People stayed married back then also. Divorce was unheard of. Yes it existed, but not that much. Now it's over 50%.

No internet dating the second you get angry with your spouse! I would stay with my uncle Sam across the street for a few weeks. He was not really my uncle Sam. I just called him that because he was that close to the family. I would eat there, see movies together, it was great. He even taught me how to drive a little in the High School parking lot. I mean really, if you get someone to feed your fish or just watch your cat for an hour these days, you're really lucky! I wrote more about Uncle Sam in chapter three.

Another thing that has been bothering me is these smart phones. Actually they are dumb phones that make you stupid, when everyone walks around like zombies. They just stare at this small screen hoping and praying that someone will text or e mail them at that very second they are looking there. I would also go to the gym and try to meet women. LA Fitness is a great place to work out and meet people, especially pretty women in great shape. Though I would walk up to them when they are working out and say "Hey, how's it going?" Then get no answer after asking two to three times. I found out later that they were not hearing me, they were listening to iTunes on the small miniscule head phones that were hidden under their hair. It drives me crazy, and others too I hear.

Why are they working out to look good and then not want to meet a nice guy? Welcome to 2014.

People need to know each other better, be a friend. When you move in, stop by and say hello. Talk to them for a few minutes at first, then an hour. Then meet their family too, if they have any. You would be amazed the things you learn, and all the food you might get. Then when you need something, the neighbor would be there for you. Wouldn't that be nice? I did get lucky and met just a few people I became friends with. Not many. Then again, I am very close to my true friends who were my neighbors thirty to forty years ago. That's just the way it was back then. The friendly family attitude, that's the way it should be. I hope it gets back like that… I really do.

* * *

What's a little neighbor? It will mean a lot if you let them in your life.

"While the spirit of neighborliness was important on the frontier because neighbors were so few, it is even more important now because our neighbors are so many." -Lady Bird Johnson

"My responsibility to myself, my neighbors, my family and the human family is to try to tell the truth." -Toni Cade Bambara

"One value that was sewn into the stitching of our character at a very early age had to do with our responsibility to help others. We were expected to be of assistance to our neighbors. Being neighborly was synonymous with being kind, friendly, and helpful to our neighbors and something that we were encouraged to do on a regular basis through firsthand experience. It was a bit like mandatory community service." -BeNeca Ward

19. THE BULLIES OF LIFE

While kids are growing up, they sometimes run into kids who they don't like. The reason is, that those unlikable kids are the ones who pick fights with the others. They are jealous and have really low self-esteem. You know who they are. Every school in every country for the last fifty years or more has had this problem. One of the most popular problems they performed was the one when they wanted my lunch money. I hated that! When you're starving and on a budget at fourteen or fifteen years old, the last thing you want is to get your money taken by those punks.

Then you go to tell your parents or, if not, the teacher and take a risk of them beating you up over a freaking dollar. This happened in the hallways of my school, and even in after-school programs like sports. Football, soccer, track, you name it. That's what happened to me. The sports bullies came to town… but it worked out well. Sort of.

I was into playing soccer as a kid. My father played when he was kid in Turkey and then my two older brothers did too, so I was hooked. I started summer soccer at nine years old… that was very young at that time. I went to see the Rochester Lancers play every year for at least a decade. But when I started playing soccer in high school, things changed. I still enjoyed it and had fun, except that I was a freshman and had to practice and sometimes play with juniors and seniors. They can be a real pain in the rear if you know what I mean. I would do drills with them and run in all kinds of weather, mostly rain. Remember that this is crappy and cold Rochester, NY in the fall and early winter! The coach would get on my nerves making me try to do the best I can do to make the team and play first string. He would scream. "PERINCHI! Run man run, don't be a punky wussie!" First string means I had to listen so I can play first when the game starts, if you don't know the terms. First... First string. I did sometimes, but not often. I would also have these guys pull pranks on me like push me in water puddles full of mud on the field. When I took a shower at the school, they would hide my towels so I would walk around soaking wet in the damn locker room. I said ..okay that's it! I don't need this anymore!. That's when my life changed...from the bullies who became cowards.

I always was the class clown in school making people laugh for as long as I remember. As early as nine years old, I would do voices and sound effects in the library. Star Trek was my favorite, especially Kirk and Scotty and the famous Transporter-phaser sounds. I also got kicked out for doing that. I didn't care because that's what I did the best. It's who I am! So, the next year I was not sure if I wanted to deal with the soccer bums, but just loved to play. Then something happened that changed my life. Well, I should say someone. His name was Adam. He was a friend who I knew my whole life so he REALLY knew Jon Pirincci. His parents knew my parents and we hung out all the time. I love to be funny and act, so he told me about the Drama Club. With the Drama Club came the Choir and of course singing and girls… lots of girls. Pretty girls.

So, now I'm thinking what the heck was I going to ACT in? I never acted in my life...nothing! Okay, maybe I said a few funny lines that I saw on Jonny Carson, but not legitimate actual lines a playwright wrote for a major play or musical. Christmas was coming and I was going to Miami for the new year. Then I found out "Fiddler on the Roof" was the next musical. So I am thinking let's try to get in the show even as a background singer, that's it, not a lead, background. Then I found out that auditions for guys in the show were being held on the same date that I was leaving to Miami with my family. So I decided to go on the night for women the night before I was scheduled to leave. I read for Mordcha the Inn Keeper and some of the other roles. It was a huge role and I even had my own scenes with the lead Tevye. I was so nervous because I have never acted in my life! Not even reading out load or with a script. I am also in the same room as the girls. I was the only guy! There is no way I was going to get this… no way!

So I go on vacation and have a great time. I tell my parents that I did the reading and that's it. I never expected anything to happen and I did not care. Okay… maybe a little because I saw some really cute girls at the audition. When I came back from Miami with a nice tan I looked at the call sheet to see if I made it on the show. Any part. I was not. Then the Musical Director came over to me and said, "Jon, congratulations on the part!" "What Part?" I said. I looked again and saw my name on the very bottom. It was a lead… one of the main leads. Mordcha the Inn Keeper!. I had pages of lines and songs to sing… in key! I was terrified. I almost said I don't want to do it. Just make me a guy in the town that's all. No lines… no singing. Ahhhh!!

Months later after dealing with the rehearsals, snowy days, long hours, after-school soccer, and a wisdom tooth taken out, the show was amazing! We had a sold out show on all nights, even the balcony. Every show! Yes I had a few of the bullies from my soccer team there. Yes they said I was a wimp and that acting was not for real men, it was for wussies and girlies....not a soccer dude. That did not bother me, not for one second. I was following my inner feeling. My gut. My internal flow of positivity and guidance. You know how that feels right? If not… read on.

I then knew at the exact time I finished my last line in my performance and heard the thundering applause, I was home. So then I knew I would have to do more the next year and the next and the next. I even went to college at Ithaca just to study theater. Which I did. I loved it.

After I finished college, I still needed that creative excitement. That's when I heard about becoming a stand-up comedian. Stand up comedy was getting really big back then and I wanted to be part of it. The problem with that was there were many comedy bullies in that field too. Saying my jokes are not funny, the timing is off, I need new impressions, on and on and on. Boy, they were wrong. Because just a few years later after honing my act and doing voices with faces, I performed with my fellow chin master. The one that got me in the comedy game. The life and breath of humor for the past 35 years, Mr. Jay Leno. It all went downhill after that. I actually met him after a comedy show at a local club in Rochester also. You can read more on this in the chapter Jay and Jon...jaws of humor.

So as I look back at my creative comedy/acting life, I saw many road blocks. People of the world who are bullies. These are the ones who don't believe in anyone...especially themselves. You must not be associated with them. You must not be around anyone who is negative in any way. Stay away because it will direct you to a life you just may not want. That is one of the worse things that can happen.

* * *

What's a little prevention and Life Road Blocks? It's NOTHING if you do not let it stop your dreams!.

"Nobody in life gets exactly what they thought were going to get. But if you work really hard and you're kind, amazing things will happen" -Conan O'Brien

"As you become more clear about who you really are, you'll be better able to decide what is best for you-the first time around" -Oprah Winfrey.

"Faith is daring to put your dream to the test. It is better to try to do something and fail than do nothing and succeed" -Robert H Schuller.

20. BONJOUR… FRANK AND RAMONE

A few weeks after Hurricane Andrew I did not know what to do with my life. I had just moved from Orlando, Florida and was in my condo that survived those devastating hurricane winds. I moved there for acting and comedy because I heard that's the place to be besides moving across the country to Los Angeles.

So then my brother Jemal called me and asked if there were a lot of houses that were destroyed or needed repairing. I was thinking "Yeah… you can say that!" My brother was a licensed contractor in Florida and wanted to come down to repair the houses there. I thought it was a great idea because I had no job and no direction or any way to make money after the hurricane. So I thought I get to work with my brother and learn a good trade also. A few days later, the bro comes and stays with my girlfriend and me. It was actually great because we would work all day and then come back late at night with dinner on the table. My girlfriend was an old fashioned Ukrainian girl and made food that was tasty and edible. The biggest problem was that the main part of Hurricane Andrew where the houses really needed work was 45 min to an hour away …one way. That's right. A two hour ride a day every day, seven days a week. That's not including traffic, which made it worse.

After a while, we got used to the traffic and really did not know where to go besides looking at a map. Even then, we did not know this part of Miami… we were beach boys per say. Most people there spoke Spanish to us also. Some parts were so Cuban that many talked like Al Pacino's Tony Montana in the hit movie Scarface. We finally drove around enough neighborhoods that we saw the places that needed work.

We also noticed that there were names and phone numbers on all the houses so the insurance companies could find the owners. I actually was the one that figured out to call the owners and see if they wanted to have us repair their home. It was like personal white pages on each house. What we found out is they did not want to repair their house, but sell it!. Now we were thinking who would buy a house that needed that much work… unless it was a great deal? It was! They collected insurance money and we offered them other money on top of what they got already. Genius!

Most did not want to stay in Miami any more or else move north to Ft. Lauderdale, Boca Raton etc. It's actually nicer up there. We got financing from some sources we found and paid cash for these, pennies on the dollar. Needless to say, we did very well buying over 15 homes in a few months time. The problem was, who will fix these houses for a reasonable price and who we can trust? That's where we found the GUYS… Frank and Ramone.

We did not know that back in 1992 there were hundreds of guys that came from all over the US and Canada to find work repairing the homes there. I met people from Alabama, Los Angeles, Boston, Philadelphia, even Arkansas with a banjo on their knee. Okay, maybe a power belt.

Then my brother and I drove around and noticed some places where there were just tents full of people. That's right, a tent city. This is where the guys I just mentioned about lived when they had nowhere else to go. That's where we found these two Canadian guys that looked like a French version of Laurel and Hardy, Martin and Lewis, even Tom and Jerry.

Frank was a tall skinny guy with a beard. Ramone was a short guy with no beard and a big nose. They both talked with these really French accents. You know like Pepe LePew from the old classic Hanna Barbera cartoons where the skunk chased the lovely cat. Well these guys were just like that except they chased American women while looking for work. So we needed a crew and went with these guys. We set them up to live in some of the houses we bought. I would pick them up every day and take them to the different sites that needed work.

They did everything from installing drywall, electricity, plumbing, painting, roofing. You name it, they did it. The only thing they needed was cash every day, beer and cigarettes. That's right cigarettes. Ramone would always talk like that.. CEE GARETTS. "Jean could you get me some BEEEER and CEE GA RETT si vous plais!"

I must have heard this 250 times over a year of working with them, but it was worth it. I know they saved us tens of thousands of dollars over the many homes they worked on for us. We would hang out after their work, eat pickled eggs with ham and cheese sandwiches and also have a few beers.

The best part of meeting these men is this. I found out that Frank came from a wealthy family in Montreal. His father was a prominent doctor. His mother was a technician for hospitals. Frank's brother was also a professor.

Ramone came from a good family. His parents owned different businesses in Montreal. Frank and Ramone knew each other and came together to Miami. They both loved to drink, smoke, and just live day by day. Frank would do weird things like often get drunk and lose his shoes while walking around from leaving a local bar. Ramone would work at a site and disappear for hours not knowing where he was. Then we would find him sleeping in the back of a room we did not repair yet. Once we found Frank sleeping under the stairs of a really bad house that got torn up with the hurricane. He just got up and said I am sorry... in his very French accent, grab a hammer and start working again. So weird, but loyal.

We had other workers along the way who helped us too, but none were the loyal men of that great country Canada. The men who we had work for us were great. Then we found out later that they really did not have to work. They did not have to travel to Miami and go through all of these life changing difficult times. Living in tents. Living in beat up old houses. Dealing with the attitudes and negative energy of surviving 150 mile per hour winds that destroyed most of south Miami back in 1992.

This is the reason they came. They both wanted to show their parents and family that they could work hard and live on their own merits. Their own strength and will power to help themselves and others. The others also happened to be their families.

You see Frank's father, the doctor, had major health issues and was getting sicker every week. Ramone had a falling out with his parents and did not want to live off of their income. Ramone was too proud for that. He just wanted to live day by day and enjoy life. Frank the same, day by day except for one thing.

Frank would send some money to his father to show his love and support. Ramone would help him too. They were best friends. They worked and played hard together. You see that takes off the pressure when you just live in a positive attitude… day by day!.

Well working with them was a very great experience for me. Not just to help them find work and help us, but to see just how little it meant to them to have to work so hard every day and night.

As we finished the last house, I needed a vacation and took my parents to Las Vegas and paid for the entire vacation. Hotel… food… air… everything. I never had a chance to do that before… ever! A few weeks after that my brother Jemal and I went to the Greek Islands and then Istanbul, Turkey for six weeks. All because of the profit we made off the houses Frank and Ramone fixed so well.

It's been 22 years since I saw them having a beer and A CEE GA RETT. I am sure they must be successful running their own businesses in Canada or maybe helping others like they helped us. They were just the nicest guys you could meet and know.

* * *

What's a little hard work? It's the meaning behind it… that's what really counts.

"Happiness is not in the mere possession of money; it lies in the joy of achievement, in the thrill of creative effort." -Franklin D. Roosevelt

"Choose a labor that you love, and you will never have to work a day in your life" -Confucius

"All labor that uplifts humanity has dignity and importance and should be undertaken with painstaking excellence." -Martin Luther King

21. LOOKING FOR THE GOOD… MAKES US STRONGER

A personal story by Toianna Wika

This is personally dedicated to fellow Treasure Coast victims of 2004 hurricanes Jeanne, Ivan, and Frances, and all hurricanes since and to come. May God bless you in your recovery.

Tragic circumstance has challenged our family's happiness and unity several times, before and since hurricanes Jeanne, Ivan, and Frances, each time requiring our willingness to start fresh.

Six years prior to the hurricanes, my husband and I were living our dream in Seattle. Then our second child was born severely brain damaged and terminally ill in 1997. Doctors told us that our son was a waste of their time, because he was a vegetable and lacked hope. He had snuggled into the crook of our arms since we first began rocking him as an infant. So, I ignored so called experts and with some success, I kept trying to help him respond.

Our community stared, whispered, and made ruthless commentary, like that he would be better off dead. Friends abandoned us. When our son turned two, we moved to Florida to pursue hyperbolic oxygen therapy, his only hope for survival. That entailed leaving our home, our church, remaining friends, family, and all that was familiar. However, the warm weather was more agreeable to him and he spent less time in the hospital. This gave us a higher quality of life.

Make a Wish refused to help our son. Still, we managed on our own to get him out camping, to Universal and Disney World, for a ride on an elephant and a moment on a bull's back in Texas, on the way to Arizona, by train, to visit grandparents.

Our son's therapy in Lauderdale by the Sea was unsuccessful, and he died. We focused the best we could on our four glorious years together. We felt terrific about having done all we could to help him until his body gave out, despite nearly everyone's discouragement.

Our son had known he was loved and wanted. We moved ninety minutes north into the dream home we found on the Inter coastal in Ft Pierce, where we enjoyed three years of watching dolphins migrate, fish jump out of the water, and some of the most awe inspiring sunrises. Still, I felt dead inside and could barely drag myself out of bed until someone advised me that if I spent my days allowing energy to drain into grieving our son's loss, our two living children would think I did not love them as much.

I prayed for help and found myself amongst Mary Kay beauty consultants, who inspired me to play with make-up, take care of myself, set goals, dream big, and laugh again, which cheered my worried kids. I resolved my life-long dislike of girls, while for the first time learning to be feminine myself. Through Mary Kay, I learned positivity. Meanwhile, after one hundred years of no hurricane action in our area, Ft. Pierce was torn apart in the 2004 hurricanes, Jeanne, Ivan, and Frances.

We had been grieving the loss of our four year old son since 2001, and honestly, in light of his loss, the hurricanes did not seem like such a big deal, despite the fact we lost most of our furniture, heirlooms, and some family pictures. We lost some things to black mold, including the ability to stay in our home, and some to people who broke into our home, once it was declared uninhabitable and stood unattended.

But you see… it was just… stuff.

After our home was condemned in 2005, we opted to leave Florida. We had not found work, and we knew reputedly that Minnesota had better schools. Within a few years in Minnesota, we had lost everything in savings and investments, after having tried to save our Florida house and hold our insurance responsible for structural damage compensation owed to us.

We were older. The economy was not great, and we could not find work. The only choice was to accept help from the state, and my family was amazed to discover the compassion of workers. We have been the recipients of numerous community acts of random kindness that has restored our faith in people, like the time someone anonymously left a Christmas tree on our front steps.

I had stopped believing in people having heart. Nowadays, my husband and I are first in line at food shelves and clothing banks. We feel both grateful for the places to go for help and proud of our willingness to accept the help. This keeps us in order to ensure our kids will be warm and well fed.

In the past couple of years, we both have had serious health issues. My husband had heart surgery to replace a heart valve, and I had a blood clot in my brain that gave me seizures, resulting in the equivalent of a stroke. Our illness and change of pace has given us opportunity to see what incredibly patient and compassionate kids we have. Our twelve year old holds our arms so we do not fall on ice, and our nineteen year old daughter took off a year from school and applied college money in an annuity to buy us a home, where we can live together.

These days, we are awestruck by the tiniest miracles, like finding a bucket of laundry detergent at the food bank or a thick winter coat for free at Joseph's Coats. Equally as fulfilling to me is watching our daughter and son's awareness of others she sees toting all of their worldly goods into fast food restaurants and her offering to buy them a meal when we have a little extra.

Our children are ahead of their wealthier peers, who are sheltered and take their privileges for granted. They are more independent and resourceful, and they appreciate receiving things they want when we can acquire them. Suffering has increased our gratitude for what we do have, our conviction that family matters most and has bound us closer together.

Our lives go on joyously, with ups and downs and unexpected gifts from God to get us through crises we cannot imagine surviving. After all this… life is good.

* * *

What's a little Materialistic life? When it comes to family, friends and health… absolutely nothing!

"Whatever doesn't kill us, makes us stronger." -Friedrich Nietzsche

"Smile at each other, smile at your wife, smile at your husband, smile at your children, smile at each other, it does not matter who it is-and all that will help you to grow up in greater love for each other." -Mother Theresa

"He is rich who is content with the least; for contentment is the wealth of nature" -Socrates

"Sooner or later we'll discover that the important moments in life are not the advertised ones, not the birthdays, the graduations, the weddings, not the goals achieved. The real milestones are less prepossessing. They come to the door of memory." -Susan Brownell Anthony

THE SCRIPTURES OF THE WIND

This next chapter is to show how the top religions of the world, Bible, Torah and the Quran, relate to the personal stories you just read. You will also notice that these scriptures and their beliefs are very much like all the other religions.

It is to prove just one thing and one thing only. That there are problems and similar issues we people have from all over the world and in all faiths.

It has been like that for over 2000 years.

It is up to you to believe in this... or not. If you do, again it shows all religions are very similar and are all great.

If you do not... then maybe just believe in a higher source or spiritual guidance.

You can also... not believe in anything, but what you want to believe in.

It is again, entirely up to you.

That is why we included just a few verses from each testament. If you want more information and proof, read the entire Bible, Torah or Quran.

Remember... your personal wind will take you and your thoughts wherever you want to go.

WHAT'S A LITTLE WIND?

No Worries

The Bible:

Mathew 6:25-34

So do not worry saying, "What shall we eat?" Or "What shall we drink?" Or "What shall we wear?" For the pagans run after these things and your heavenly Father knows that you need them. But seek first his kingdom and his righteousness and all these things will be given to you as well.

Therefore do not worry about tomorrow for tomorrow will worry about itself. Each day has enough trouble of its own.

The Torah:

Sieon ben Lakish, Lamantations Rabbah 2.3

Jews are this first to feel universal disaster or joy.

Shebatai ben marinus, Talmud: Betza 32 b

Whoever is merciful is certainly of the children of Abraham.

Hiya ben Abba, Deuteronomy Rabaah 3.4

Jews are characterized by modesty, mercy, and benevolence.

The Quran:

Umat ibn alkhattab

No amount of guilt can change the past and no amount of worrying can change the future, go easy on yourself, for the outcome of all affairs is determined by Allah's decree. If something is meant to go elsewhere, it will never come your way, but if its yours by destiny, from it you cannot flee.

THE CURRENT OF LIFE

Spiritual Guidance

The Bible:

Jeremiah 29:11

For I know the plans I have for you, declares the Lord. plans for welfare and not for evil, to give you a future and a hope.

Ephesians 1:11

In him we have obtained an inheritance, having been predestined according to the purpose of him who works all things according to the counsel of his will.

The Torah:

Deuteronomy 30:19

I have set before you life and death, blessing and cursing: therefore choose life, that both thou and thy seed may live.

Deuteronomy 30:20

To love the lord… that is your life and length of days.

The Quran:

9:51

Nothing will happen to us except what Allah has decreed for us. He is our protector and on Allah let the believers put their trust.

7:188

Say: For myself I have no power to benefit, nor power to hurt, save that which Allah willeth. Had I knowledge of the unseen, I should have abundance of wealth, and adversity would not touch me. I am but a warner, and a bearer of good tidings unto folk who believe.

UNCLE SAM

Patriotism

The Bible:

I John 4.20

He that sayeth he loveth God and hatest his brother is a liar. Whether in the days of Joseph or in the days of David or in the days of any of the Godly patriots such as Daniel, Isaiah, Jeremiah, or even in our day, a man who truly loves God will not set himself the task of undermining his nation or bringing railing accusations against the duly constituted and appointed authority in our land.

Ephesians 1:11

In him we have obtained an inheritance, having been predestined according to the purpose of him who works all things according to the counsel of his will.

The Talmud:

For the sake of peace one may lie, but peace itself should never be a lie.

Never expose yourself unnecessarily to danger; a miracle may not save you...and if it does, it will be deducted from your share of luck or merit.

Whoever destroys a single life is as guilty as though he had destroyed the whole world, and whoever rescues a single life earns as much merit as though he had rescued the world.

The Quran:

Islam does not forbid a muslim to love his homeland or the country in which he loves or grew up. What is reprehensible is basing ones feelings of loyalty and disavowal on that, and loving the hating on that basis. A person who belongs to the same country as you is not closer to you than a Muslim from another land, and the reason for your loving or hating others should not be whether or not they come from the same country as you. Rather loyalty and disavowal or love and hatred, should all be based on Islam and piety.

THE NUMBERS THAT CHANGED LIVES

Prejudice

The Bible:

Galatians 3:28

There is neither Jew nor Greek, There is neither slave nor free, there is no male and female, for you are all one in Christ Jesus.

Galatians 7:1

Judge not, that you be not judged.

Galatians 16:7

But the Lord said to Samuel: Do not look on his appearance or on the height of his stature, because I have rejected him. For the Lord sees not as man sees: man looks on the outward appearance, but the Lord looks on the heart.

The Torah:

Jonathan ben Elazar. Talmud: Yebmot 109b

A judge should always visualize a sword suspended over him, and Gehenna (hell) gaping under him.

Talmud: Sanhedrin 31a

A judge is a "Talebearer" if after a case is concluded, he says "I was for acquittal but my colleagues were for conviction"

Zohar, Exodus 257a

A judge sins if he looks not for merits in the accused

The Quran:

Al-An'am 6:159

As for those who divide their religion and break up into sects, thou hast no part in them in the least" their affair is with Allah. He will in the end tell them the truth of all that they did.

Al'Anfal 8:46

And obey Allah and his messenger :and fall into disputes, lest ye lose heart and your power depart, and be patient and preserving: For Allah is with those who patiently preserve.

THE BIRD AND THE CHAIR

Spirits and Passings

The Bible:

John 4:1

Beloved, do not believe every spirit, but test the spirits to see whether they are from God, for many false prophets have gone out into the world.

Ecclesiastes 9:5

For the living know that they shall die: but the dead know not any thing, neither have they any more a reward; for the memory of them is forgotten.

Deuteronomy 18:11

There shall not be found among you any one who maketh his son or his daughter to pass through the fire, or who useth divination, or an observer of times, or an enchanter, or a witch, or a charmer, or a consulter with familiar spirits, or a wizard, or a necromancer.
For all who do these things are an abomination unto the Lord, and because of these abominations the Lord thy God doth drive them out from before thee.

Philippians 1:23-24

I am hard pressed between the two. My desire is to depart and be with Christ, for that is far better. But to remain in the flesh is more necessary on your account.

The Torah:

Daniel 12:2

"Many of those that sleep in the dust of the earth will awake, some to eternal life, others to reproaches, to everlasting abhorrence"--implies that resurrection will be followed by a day of judgment. Those judged favorably will live forever and those judged to be wicked will be punished.

Mishneh Torah, Repentance 8

In the world to come, there is nothing corporeal, and no material substance; there are only souls of the righteous without bodies -- like the ministering angels... The righteous attain to a knowledge and realization of truth concerning God to which they had not attained while they were in the murky and lowly body.

Sanhedrin 10:1

All Israelites have a share in the world-to-come... [However], these are they that have no share in the world-to-come: one who says there is no resurrection of the dead prescribed in the Torah, and that the Torah is not from Heaven, and an Epicurean.

The Quran:

The faithful do not die: perhaps they become translated from this perishable world to the world of eternal existences.

Death is a blessing to a Muslim. Remember and speak well of your dead, and refrain from speaking ill of them.

Death is a bridge that uniteth friend with friend.

TRUE LOVE... KISMET

Marriage

The Bible:

Colossians 3:18-19

Wives, submit to your husbands, as is fitting in the Lord. Husbands, love your wives and do not be harsh with them.

Hebrews 13:4-7

Marriage should be honored by all, and the marriage bed kept pure, for God will judge the adulterer and all the sexually immoral.

Keep your lives free from the love of money and be content with what you have, because God has said : "Never will I leave you: never will I forsake you"

The Torah:

Rabbi Moshe Maimonides- Hilchot Ishut 15:19

Honor your wife more than yourself. Love her like yourself. Lavish money on her according to your means. Don't make her afraid of you. Speak gently to her. Don't be sad or cross.

Zohar

When a soul is sent from heaven, it contains both male and female characteristics, the male elements enter the boy baby, the female, the girl baby, and if they be worthy, God reunites them in marriage.

24.32

You should encourage those of you who are single to get married. They may marry the righteous among your male and female servants, if they are poor. God will enrich them from his grace. God is Bounteous, Knower.

The Quran:

25:74

And they say, "Our Lord, let our spouses and children be a source of joy for us, and keep us in the forefront of the righteous."

40:8

Our Lord, and admit them into the gardens of Eden that You promised for them and for the righteous among their parents, spouses, and children. You are the Almighty, Most Wise.

A SURVIVOR OF FAITH

Guardian Angels

The Bible:

Exodus 23:20

Behold, I send an Angel before thee, to keep thee in the way, and to bring thee into the place which I have prepared.

Psalms 103:20

Bless the LORD, ye his angels, that excel in strength, that do his commandments, hearkening unto the voice of his word.

Matthew 24:31

And he shall send his angels with a great sound of a trumpet, and they shall gather together his elect from the four winds, from one end of heaven to the other.

The Torah:

Genesis Rabbah 50.2

One angel does not perform two missions, nor is one mission performed by two angels.

Jonathan ben Elazar (Talmud: Hagiga 14a)

From each utterance of the Holy One an angel is born.

Maimonides, Guide for the Perplexed, 1900, 2.6

Every one entrusted with a mission is an angel...All forces that reside in the body are angels.

The Quran:

Surat an-Nahl, 32

Those the angels take in a virtuous state. They say, 'Peace be upon you! Enter the Garden for what you did.

Surat az-Zumar, 73

And those who guard against evil of their Lord will be driven to the Garden in companies and when they arrive there, finding its gates open, its custodians will say to them, 'Peace be upon you! You have done well so enter it timelessly, for ever.'

Surah Qaf, 16-18

We created man and We know what his own self whispers to him. We are nearer to him than his jugular vein. And the two recording angels are recording, sitting on the right and on the left. He does not utter a single word, without a watcher by him, pen in hand!

Surat ar-Ra'd, 11

Everyone has a succession of angels in front of him and behind him, guarding him by Allah's command. Allah never changes a people's state until they change what is in themselves. When Allah desires evil for a people, there is no averting it. They have no protector apart from Him.

THE FRIENDLY... CON MAN

Faith

The Bible:

Mathew 17:20

He Replied: "Because you have so little faith. I tell you the truth, if you have faith as small as a mustard seed, you can say to this mountain, Move from here to there and it will move. Nothing will be impossible for you."

The Torah:

Maimonides. Commentary to Mishna: Sanhedrin, 1168, 10.1, Thirteen Principles #12

I believe with perfect faith in the coming of the Messiah; and although he tarry, I will wait daily for his coming.

Abram in Genesis 12

Furthermore, the stories of Abraham, Isaac, and Jacob and Exodus 1-18 (the first two-thirds of Moses' life) occur before the giving of the Law. Thus Abraham and the patriarchs are portrayed as people of faith who lived without the Law, and Moses is a person who lived part of his life without the Law and part of his life under the Law.

The Quran:

A man who has faith in Allah does not worry when the world tries to pull him down because he knows Allah's hand is holding him up.

MY HEAVELY DOG

Companionship

The Bible:

Ecclesiastes 3:18-21

As for humans, God tests them so that they may see that they are like the animals. Surely the fate of human beings is like that of the animals, the same fate awaits them both. As one dies, so does the other. All have the same breath(literally "Spirit"),humans have no advantage over animals. Everything is meaningless. All go to the same place, all come from dust, and to dust all return. Who knows if the human spirit rises upward and if the spirit of the animal goes down to earth.

The Torah:

Talmud: Shabbat 128b

Prevention of suffering of animals is biblical law, and therefore takes precedence of all rabbinical laws (E.g. rabbinical laws relating to the Sabbath may be broken in order to prevent an animal from suffering)

Histapkhuth Ha-nefesh,R Nachman Bratzlaver, pg. 4B

Both a man and an animal receive the necessaries for their existence. The difference, however, lies in this: that a man is able to ask God to meet his needs. Be therefore a man! Ask God for everything you need.

The Quran:

Verily there are heavenly rewards for any act of kindness to live animal.

Verily one hundred loving kindnesses: One of which hath sent down amongst man, quadrupeds and every moving thing upon the face of the earth, be it they are kind to each other and forgive each other.

THE MOTHER'S DECISION

Children

The Bible:

Proverbs 31:25-30

Strength and dignity are her clothing, and she laughs at the time to come. Her children rise up and call her blessed; her husband also, and he praises her: "Many women have done excellently, but you surpass them all."

Isaiah 9:15

Can a woman forget her nursing child, that she should have no compassion on the son of her womb? Even these may forget, yet I will not forget you.

Psalm 12:27:3

Behold, children are a heritage from the Lord, the fruit of the womb a reward

The Torah:

Isaiah 66:13

As a mother comforts her child, so will I comfort you; and you will be comforted over Jerusalem.

Proverbs 31:10

A wife of noble character who can find? She is worth far more than rubies.

Proverbs 31:29

Many women do noble things, but you surpass them all.

The Quran:

"Heaven lie at the feet of mothers."
O messenger of God! Verily have I done a great crime: is there any act by which I

may repent.? He said, "Have you a mother?" "No" said the questioner. "Have you an aunt?" asked Muhammad. He said "Yes I have," Muhammad said "Go, do good to her, and your crime will be pardoned."

THINK... SEE... AND BELIEVE

Positive Belief

The Bible:

Philippians 4.8

Finally, Brothers, whatever is true, whatever is honorable, what ever is just, whatever is pure, what ever is lovely, whatever is commendable, if there is any excellence, if there is anything worthy of praise, think about these things.

Philippians 4.6

Do not be anxious about anything, but in everything by prayer and supplication with thanksgiving let your requests be made known to God.

The Torah:

Akiba Mishma: Avot 3:15

All is foreseen, yet man is endowed in free will.

Huna, Talmud: Makkot 10b

The man is led the way he wishes to follow.

23:111

Indeed, I have rewarded them this day for their patience, they are indeed the ones who are successful.

The Quran:

12:87

And never give up hope of Allah's soothing mercy. Truly no one despairs of Allahs soothing Mercy except those who have no faith

THE X MAN ROOMMATE

Health is Wealth

The Bible:

Corinthians 6:19.20

Or do you not know that your body is a temple of the Holy Spirit. With in you, whom you have from God? You are not your own, for you were bought with a price. So glorify God in your body.

Corinthians 10:31

So, whether you eat or drink, or whatever you do, do all to the Glory of God.

John 1.2

Beloved, I pray that all may go well with you and that you may be in good health, as it goes well with your soul.

The Torah:

Respect your own body as the receptacle, messenger, and instrument of the spirit. Rabbi Samson Raphael Hirsch, The Nineteen Letters (1836), no. 11

Apocrypha of Ben Sira, 30:16

There is no wealth like health.

R. Tanhum bar Hiyya in Midrash B'reishit/Genesis Rabbah 1:3

If a gourd has a hole as tiny as a needle's eye, all its air escapes; Yet man, with so many cavities and orifices, retains his breath. Verily, "You do wonders!" (Psalms 86:10)

The Quran:

4:79

Everything good that happens to you (O Man) is from God, everything bad that happens to you is from your own actions.

10:57

O Mankind: There has come to you a direction from your Lord and a healing for the (disease) in your hearts - and for those who believe a guidance and mercy!

17:82

And We sent down in the Quran that which is healing and a mercy to those who believe: to the unjust it causes nothing but loss after loss.

HE'S GOOD PEOPLE

Faith and Friends

The Bible:

Psalms 37:7-9

Rest in the Lord, and wait patiently for him: Fret not thyself because of him who prospereth in his way, because of the man who bringeth wicked devices to pass.

James 5:7

Be patient therefore brethren, unto the coming of the Lord. Behold, the husband man waiteth for the precious fruit of the earth, and hath long patience for it, until he receive the early and latter rain.

The Torah:

Ibn Gabriol, Choice of Pearls

My friend is he who will tell me my faults in private.

Ibn Gabriol

There are three types of friends: those like food, without which you can't live; those like medicine, which you need occasionally; and those like an illness, which you never want.

Pirke de Rabbi Eliezer 34

A man has three friends: his sons, his wealth, and his good deeds.

The Quran:

16:127

Be patient, for your patience is with the help of Allah.

41:35

No one will be granted such goodness except those who exercise patience and self - constraint, none but persons of the greatest good fortune

THE NO-HOME MAN

Compassion

The Bible:

Proverbs 19.47

He who is gracious to a poor man lends to the Lord, And he will repay him for his good deed.

Corinthians 12:25-26

That there should be no division in this body, but that the members should have the same care for one another. And if one member suffers, all the members suffer with it, if one member is honored, all the members rejoice with it.

Peter 3:8

To sum upset all be harmonious. Sympathetic brotherly, kindhearted, and humble in spirit.

The Torah:

Shulchan Aruch, Yoreh Deah 249:3 Shul

A person should give pleasantly, joyously, with a good heart, showing sympathy for the poor, sharing in his sense of pain and sorrow.

Shulchan Aruch, Yoreh Deah 249:5

If a person convinces others to give, his reward is even greater than when simply giving by himself.

Shulchan Aruch, Yoreh Deah 249:13

One should not be arrogant when giving.

The Quran:

On those who believe and do good deeds of righteousness there is no blame for what they ate (in the past) when they guard themselves from evil, and believe, and do deeds of righteousness- (or) again, guard them selves from evil and believe-(or) again, guard them selves from evil and do good. For Allah loveth those who do good.

Al-Quari

Then, he who whose balance (of good deeds) will be (found) heavy. Will be in a life of good pleasure and satisfaction.

Al-Ankaboot, Chapter 29, Verse 58

But those who believe and work deeds of righteousness- to them shall We give a home in Heaven-lofty mansions beneath which flow rivers-to dwell there in aye-an excellent reward for those who do (good)!

HONESTY... FOR LIFE

Honesty

The Bible:

Hebrews 13.5

Keep your life free from love of money, and be content with what you have, for he said "I will never leave you nor forsake you."

Proverbs 22:1-29

A good name is to be chosen rather than great riches, and favor is better than silver or Gold. The rich and poor meet together, the Lord is the maker of them all. The prudent sees danger and hides himself, but the simple go on and suffer for it. The reward for humility and fear of the Lord is riches and honor and life. Thorns and snares are in the way of the crooked, whoever guards his soul will keep far from them.

The Torah:

Elizer ben Philo.Mishna:toheret 7.9

A woman of valor can find? Her price is far above rubies.

Joseph.Talmud:shabbat 62a

Woman are a distant race.

The Quran:

Saheeh Al-Bukhari

Honesty descended from the heavens and settled in the roots of the hearts of men (Faithful believers) and then the Quran was revealed and the people read the Quran (and learnt from it) and also learnt from the sayings and traditions.

JAY AND JON... THE JAWS OF HUMOR

Jealousy

The Bible:

3:16

For where jealousy and selfish ambition exist, there will be disorder and every vile practice.

4:2-3

You desire and do not have, so you murder. You covet and cannot obtain, so you fight and quarrel. You do not have, because you do not ask. You ask and do not receive, because you ask wrongly, to spend it on your passions.

3:14

But if you have bitter jealousy and selfish ambition in your hearts, do not boast and be false to the truth.

The Torah:

Bible: Cant. 8.6
Jealousy is as cruel as the grave.

Proverb. q Dimi of Nehardea, Talmud Baba Batra: 21a
The jealousy of scribes increases wisdom.

Zohar: Genesis 245a
Love without jealousy is not true love.

The Quran:

That man desires that the comfort enjoyed by his fellow Muslim brother may be taken away from the his even if thereby he himself does not get any benefit. This is the worst kind of jealousy. Sometimes man does not want that someone's ease may be taken away from him but wants the same ease for himself, and since it does not reach him, he entertains a desire for the other man's down fall and possibly, if he gets such strength, he removes the said ease from the other person. His heart would feel happy if the other prosperity vanishes but, at the same, he is also angry with his own heart due to such wish and also condemns scolds it.

NEIGHBORS

Loving Your Neighbor

The Bible:

Mark 12:31

You shall love your neighbor as yourself. There is no other commandment greater than these.

Proverbs 3.29

Do not plan evil against your neighbor, who dwells trustingly beside you.

Mathew 7:12

So whatever you wish that others would do to you, do also to them, for this is the law and the prophets.

The Torah:

Thou shalt love thy neighbor as thyself: R. Akiva said: This is the fundamental principle of the Torah. Ben Azai said: This is the book of the generations of man (Gen. 5:1) transcends the weight of that.

Bereshit Rabba 24, 7 elaborates:

Do not say, since I was shamed let my neighbor be similarly shamed, since I was cursed. Said R. Tanhuma: If you act thus, know whom you are shaming – in the likeness of God made He him (Gen. 5:1).

Love thy neighbor as thyself – only if he is – your neighbor, i.e. virtuous but not if he is wicked, as it is written, the fear of the Lord is to hate evil (Prov.8:13)

The Quran:

The best person in Gods sight is the best amongst his friends, and the best of neighbors near God is the best person in his own neighborhood. A Muslim who mixeth with people and putteth up with their inconveniences, is better than one who doth not mix with them, and bear patience. Do you love your creator? Love your fellow beings first.

BULLIES OF LIFE

Bad Company

The Bible:

Corinthians 15:33

Do not be deceived: "Bad company ruins good morals."

Proverbs 13:20

Whoever walks with the wise becomes wise, but the companion of fools will suffer harm.

Psalm 1.1:1

Blessed is the man who walks not in the counsel of the wicked, nor stands in the way of sinners, nor sits in the seat of scoffers.

The Torah:

Proverbs 3:27

Do not withhold the good from them to whom it is due, when it is in the power of thine hand to do it.

Psalm 34:15

Depart from evil and do good; seek peace, and pursue it.

Talmud: Kiddushin 40a

Happy is he who performs a good deed: for he may tip the scales for himself and the world.

The Quran:

49:11

O you who have believed, let not a people ridicule [another] people; perhaps they may be better than them; nor let women ridicule [other] women; perhaps they may be better than them. And do not insult one another and do not call each other by [offensive] nicknames. Wretched is the name of disobedience after [one's] faith. And whoever does not repent - then it is those who are the wrongdoers.

FRANK AND RAMONE… THE WORKERS

Life's Work

The Bible:

Thessalonians 3:10-12

For even when we were with you, we would give you this command: If anyone is not willing to work, let him not eat. For we hear that some among you walk in idleness, not busy at work, but busy bodies. Now such persons we command and encourage in the Lord Jesus Christ to do their work quietly and to earn their own living.

The Torah:

Jacob.Midrash tehillim 23.3

Only manual work can make you blessed.(Deut. 2.7)

Judah ben Bathyra.Avot de rabbi Nathan,ch 11

If you have no regular work, find something to do-perhaps in a neglected yard or field.

The Quran:

Therefore, Islam is a religion of worshiping the creator, with an essential part of that being working for survival. God tells us in the Quran to traverse the universe and make use of all the abundant resources that have been created for us.

Albani, Series of weak and fabricated hadiths

Work hard(for making a living and survival) as if you are going to die. Prophet Muhammad made it clear that getting ones sustenance from ones work is one of the praise worthy acts of worship. It is recorded in his traditions how he turned a man who came to him begging into a productive member of society by teaching him how to work and provide for him self.

LOOKING FOR THE GOOD MAKES US STRONGER

Material Possessions

The Bible:

Hebrews 13:5

Keep your life free from love of money, and be content with what you have, for he has said, "I will never leave you nor forsake you."

Luke 12:15

And he said to them, "Take care, and be on your guard against all covetousness, for one's life does not consist in the abundance of his possessions."

Timothy 6:10

For the love of money is a root of all kinds of evils. It is through this craving that some have wandered away from the faith and pierced themselves with many pangs.

Mathew 6:33

But seek first the kingdom of God and his righteousness, and all these things will be added to you.

Mathew 6.24

No one can serve two masters, for either he will hate the one and love the other, or he will be devoted to the one and despise the other. You cannot serve God and money.

The Torah:

Book of Proverbs 28:6

Better is the poor that walketh in his uprightness, than he that is perverse in his ways, though he be rich.

Book of Proverbs 16:16

How much better it is to get wisdom than gold! and to get understanding rather to be chosen than silver.

The Quran:

3: 92

Never will you attain the good until you spend from that which you love. And whatever you spend-indeed, Allah is knowing of it.

Riches are not from the Abundance of worldly goods, but from a contented mind.

"It is difficult, for a man laden with riches, to climb the steep path leadeth to bliss."

FINAL WORD

I hope you enjoyed my book and it created "Winds of Change" in your life, like it did mine. Please share this with your family and friends, and spread the positive breeze of your life to help others. I look forward to seeing you in person and let me share my life stories with you.

To learn more, please visit:
www.whatsalittlewind.com

You can contact Jon and his staff at:
whatsalittlewind@gmail.com

Thanks again and God Bless.
Jon Pirincci

ABOUT THE AUTHOR

Jon Pirincci has been entertaining in many different areas for the past 40 years. It started in Rochester, NY, impersonating people he knew in school. Then he started on his parents and relatives, followed by well-known TV stars and even cartoon characters.

That started his Stand Up comedy career, traveling from New York to Miami, then Los Angeles. He performed his act with some of the top comedians in the country, including Jay Leno (he was on the Tonight Show), Andrew Dice Clay, and even Billy Gardell from the hit series "Mike and Molly" with Melissa McCarthy. JP also performed with many other comics from David Letterman, Jimmy Kimmel, Craig Ferguson, and many more.

One of his highlights was working with Ellen DeGeneres on two national commercials, "American Express" and "JCPenney".

Jon also recently finished working on the Warner Bros. feature film "Jersey Boys", directed by Clint Eastwood and starring Christopher Walken.

Jon is also proud to have his book in Barnes and Noble bookstores nationwide.

"Thank you for breezing through my life stories and a few others. Remember one thing… you just never know where the wind will take you, so keep the sailing of your life positive." Jon

18556417R00079

Made in the USA
San Bernardino, CA
20 January 2015